To Hell or Barbados
The Ethnic Cleansing of Ireland

Sean O'Callaghan was born in Killavullen, County Cork, on 22 May 1918; educated at Wallstown National School and the Christian Brothers' School, Doneraile, and later at the Military College, Curragh, County Kildare. He was commissioned in 1936 and served in Cork and later in Dublin with the Regiment of Pearse, becoming second in command to Vivion de Valera in 1940 and serving under him in Greystones, County Wicklow.

On leaving the army he became a journalist in Fleet Street working on the *Dispatch*, the *Chronicle* and *John O'London's Weekly*. In 1952, he went to work on the *East African Standard* in Nairobi as roving correspondent, covering events in Sudan, Ethiopia, Eritrea, Rhodesia and South Africa.

In 1956, after the publication of his first book, *The Easter Lily*, he became a full-time writer.

Between 1956 and 1992, Sean O'Callaghan wrote fourteen books, many of them of an investigative nature. One, *The Slave Trade*, dealing with modern slavery in Africa and the Middle East, was translated into thirteen languages and sold in hardback and paperback over 100,000 copies. A full-length feature film was made of it by Malenotti of Rome.

Included in the books published were two other books on Ireland, *The Jackboot in Ireland* and *Execution*. The first part of an autobiography, *Down by the Glenside*, was published by Mercier Press, Cork, in 1992.

Sadly, he died as this book was going to press, in August 2000.

ACKNOWLEDGEMENTS

Many people have encouraged and helped me in the writing of this book. Chief among them I would single out Michael Carroll, M.A. of Bantry; Professor Kenneth L. Carroll of Maryland; C.F.J. MacCarthy (historian) of Cork; Ulick O'Connor; Gregory O'Connor, Archivist of National Archives, Dublin; Peter Simmonds, Ronald Taylor, Mrs Betty Carillo Shannon and, above all, Patrick Kelman Roach, all of Barbados. Patrick Roach was my guide and mentor there. Finally, thanks to Desiree Brincat and Yvonne Magri for typing the manuscript, as well as my wife, Halina, and son, Mark, for their advice, support and help.

To one and all, I owe a deep debt of gratitude.

Sean O'Callaghan
Malta, July 2000

SEAN O'CALLAGHAN

TO HELL OR BARBADOS

The ethnic cleansing of Ireland

A Brandon Paperback

First published in 2000 by Brandon
This paperback edition published in 2001 by
Brandon
an imprint of Mount Eagle Publications
Dingle, Co. Kerry, Ireland

10 9 8 7 6 5 4 3 2 1

British Library Cataloguing in Publication Data is available
for this book.

ISBN 0 86322 287 0

Cover design by id communications, Tralee, Co. Kerry
Typesetting by Red Barn Publishing, Skeagh, Skibbereen
Printed by The Guernsey Press, Channel Islands

To the Irish men, women and children
who lie in unhallowed ground
in the sugar cane fields of Barbados

Contents

Acknowledgements

Introduction   9

Chapter One: The Effusion of Blood   11

Chapter Two: The Rape of Wexford   27

Chapter Three: Transplantation   41

Chapter Four: The Ethnic Cleansing of Ireland   55

Chapter Five: The Irish in Barbados   65

Chapter Six: The Irish White Slave Trade   77

Chapter Seven: The Slavery of Sugar   89

Chapter Eight: Sugar Plantations   97

Chapter Nine: The Irish *Via Dolorosa*   111

Chapter Ten: Revolts and Rebellions   123

Chapter Eleven: The Cabbage Stalk Soldiers   131

Chapter Twelve: The Irish in Jamaica   145

Chapter Thirteen: The Irish in America   161

Chapter Fourteen: The Irish Buccaneers   171

Chapter Fifteen: The Irish and the Quakers   189

Chapter Sixteen: The Restoration and its Aftermath   201

Chapter Seventeen: The Red Legs of Barbados   207

Chapter Eighteen: The Red Legs Today   215

Bibliography   227

Index   233

"*Few, but readers of Old Colonial Papers and records are aware that a lively trade was carried on between England and the Plantations, as the Colonies were then called, from 1647 to 1690, in political prisoners, where they were sold by auction to the Colonists for various terms of years, sometimes for life.*"
Colonel A.B. Ellis,
"White Slaves and Bond Servants in the Plantations" (1883)

"*Those sold to the heretics in America are treated by them more cruelly than the slaves under the Turks; nor is any attention paid to youth or the decrepitude of old age, to sex or rank, to sacerdotal orders, to religious life.*"
Cardinal Giovanni Battista Rinuccini, papal nuncio to the Confederation of Kilkenny (1645–48)

"*When slavery is established in any part of the world, those who are free are by far the most proud and jealous of their freedom.*"
Edmund Burke, Irish statesman and orator (1729–97)

INTRODUCTION

Writing a book on the ethnic cleansing of Ireland in the seventeenth century is a daunting task. Although the expression itself is modern, it applies well to the wholesale transportation of Irish men, women and children who were sold into slavery in Barbados and North America.

I had written books on slavery previously. *The Slave Trade* dealt with slavery in the Sudan, which is still taking place. The books I wrote on the white and yellow slave trades dealt with girls' being sold into prostitution in Europe and the Far East. The collapse of the Iron Curtain has greatly increased the trade in Europe. In the Far East, female children and young girls are still a disposable commodity. Writing about Irish slavery is a different matter. So little material is available on the subject that we do not even know the numbers of people transported. One historian, the Reverend Aubrey Gwynn, SJ, who did considerable research on the subject in the 1930s, estimated that over 50,000 men, women and children were transported to Barbados and Virginia between 1652–59.

What became of them? Although I am not a historian, I determined to find out. There are no Irish records. They were destroyed when the Public Records Office in Dublin was burned in 1922.

The State Papers in the English Public Records Office in Kew yielded some information, as did the Shipping Register of the period, giving details of some of the ships engaged in the transportation as well as the names of their masters, but this was not enough. Did any records exist of the people transported or of their lives in the sugar fields of Barbados or in the tobacco fields of Virginia? One thing is certain, there is no record of any having ever returned, nor of any account of their sufferings.

I felt the answer must be in Barbados. I wrote to the librarian of the Barbados Museum and Historical Society. Three weeks later I received a reply from Mrs Betty Shannon, the librarian. In a letter she informed me that the library contained a quantity of files on Irish, Scottish and African slaves. It was more than I could have hoped for. I left for Barbados in August 1993. This book is the result.

CHAPTER ONE

The Effusion of Blood

> *"I am persuaded that this is a righteous judgement of God upon these barbarous wretches, who have imbrued their hands in so much innocent blood and that it will tend to prevent the effusion of blood for the future."*
> Letter written by Oliver Cromwell after Drogheda (1649)

THE CIVIL WAR in England was over. Many of the vanquished Cavaliers lay in jails and lock-ups, there to await transportation to Barbados. After the execution of Charles I and the ending of the monarchy, a new republic was established with Oliver Cromwell as first president of its Council of State. Its forty members were mainly merchants, with a sprinkling of lawyers and army officers.

Many problems faced the new Commonwealth. There was discontent in the country and problems with the army, including a mutiny in Banbury and at Salisbury among the troops destined for Ireland. This mutiny was quelled by Cromwell and Sir Thomas Fairfax, who had three of the ringleaders shot.

Cromwell's greatest preoccupation, however, was with Ireland. Since the beheading of the king and resignation of the royalist lord lieutenant of Ireland, James Butler, Earl of

11

Ormonde, his greatest fear was that all classes of Irishman, Protestant and Catholic alike, would unite to invade England.

> If we do not endeavour to make good our interest there, and that timely, we shall not only have . . . our interest rooted out there, but they will in a very short time be able to land forces in England and to put us to trouble here. . . I had rather be overrun with a Cavalierish interest than a Scotch interest; I had rather be overrun with a Scotch interest than an Irish; and I think of all this is most dangerous. If they shall be able to carry on their work, they will make this the most miserable people in the earth, for all the world knows their barbarism.

This amply shows Cromwell's frame of mind before leaving for Ireland. His fear was that the young Charles, who had been declared king in Scotland immediately after his father's death, would land in Ireland, rally the people to the royalist cause and lead an invasion to England. In the summer of 1649 it seemed to Cromwell that Ireland had become a royalist state and the prospects of a successful English invasion of that country were receding with every passing day.

On 15 March 1649 the Council of State nominated him to command the troops for the invasion of Ireland. Cromwell hesitated for several reasons. In the first place his health had not been good since the previous Christmas, when he had a breakdown. He was also determined that he should have a free hand in Ireland and that the forces under his command would be properly equipped and provided for as he did not want soldiers to follow him out of personal loyalty. Finally, on 30 March, he accepted the nomination, saying that: "It matters not who is our commander-in-chief if God be so."

All was now set for the invasion of Ireland and the reconquest of a country from the "barbarous wretches" who had spilled "so much innocent blood" in the rebellion of 1641. In 1641, eight years before his invasion of Ireland, the Irish rose in rebellion against the English and Scottish planters who had seized their lands during the Elizabethan plantations. The rebellion began in Ulster, which was the most heavily planted, and soon spread throughout the country until only Dublin and Derry remained in English hands. At the beginning of this rebellion only peasants took part, armed with pikes and pitchforks. They fell upon the settlers, killing men, women and children indiscriminately.

Sir John Temple, who was in Dublin Castle at the time the rebellion broke out, wrote in his *History of the Horrid Rebellion in Ireland* (1646): "The crisis burst upon us with the suddenness of a violent torrent..." He claimed that the rebels, inflamed by Jesuits, did "march on furiously destroying all the English, sparing neither sex nor age, most barbarously murdering them, and that with greater cruelty than was ever used among Turks or Infidels".

Sir John Temple gave the figure of those killed as 100,000; Dr Bate, a royalist who later changed sides to become Cromwell's personal physician, described the Irish as "a mixed rabble, part papist and part savages, guilty in the highest degree of all those crimes", and gave the number of settlers slain as 200,000. W.E. Lecky's *History of Ireland*, published in the middle of the eighteenth century, gave the number of those killed as 4000, which is today accepted as being closer to the true figure.

King Charles I believed the exaggerated accounts of the massacre and accompanying atrocities committed by the Irish and instructed his forces in Ireland "to prosecute the Rebels and Traitors with fire and sword". He also sent a message to Parliament that he intended to put himself at the head of an army and go to Ireland "to chastise those wicked and detestable rebels, odius to God and all good men". Parliament replied that it would consider his departure from England equal to a formal abdication of the throne. Charles stayed. Bulstrode Whitelocke, a member of the House, said that the Irish would be rooted out by a new and overwhelming plantation of English and that another England would be speedily found in Ireland. The Lords of the Council ordered Lord Ormonde, then lieutenant general of the army in Ireland, "to burn, spoil, waste, consume, destroy and demolish all the places, towns and houses where the said rebels are . . . and to kill and destroy all the men there inhabiting able to bear arms".

That there were massacres of Protestants by Catholics in the early days of the rebellion cannot be denied; they were perpetrated by the peasantry whose hatred for the settlers was endemic. The leaders of the rebellion, Rory O'Moore, Lord Maguire, Sir Phelim O'Neill and others, soon brought them under control. It was not what actually happened that mattered, however, but what the English believed had taken place.

The Irish seemed, to Englishmen of that time, of a lower race. To Cromwell it was to be a contest between the honest English and the murderous and treacherous Irish. Pamphlets published before and during the English Civil War fuelled the hatred of the English for the Irish. They were depicted as a subhuman species, undeserving of pity or mercy. An extract from one of these pamphlets is sufficient to show the virulence of the hatred that the Puritans had for the Irish people:

> These Irish, anciently called Anthropophagi (man-eaters), have a tradition among them, that when the devil showed our Saviour all the kingdoms of the earth and their glory he would not show him Ireland, but reserved it for himself . . . They are the very offal of men, dregs of mankind, reproach of Christendom, the bots that crawl on the beast's tail . . .
>
> I beg upon my hands and knees that the expedition against them may be undertaken whilst the hearts and hands of our soldiery are hot. To whom I will be bold to say briefly: Happy is he who shall

> reward them as they have served us; and cursed is he
> that shall do the work of the Lord negligently. Cursed
> be he that holdeth back his sword from blood; yea,
> cursed be he that maketh not his sword drunk with
> Irish blood.

Many Irish soldiers crossed over to England and took part on the king's side during the Civil War. On 24 October 1644, Parliament passed an ordinance that "no quarter shall henceforth be given to any Irishman or papist born in Ireland captured on land or at sea". In the same year a Captain Swanley, a naval officer fighting for Parliament, captured a ship out of Dublin bound for Bristol with seventy Irish soldiers and two women aboard. He threw them all overboard, tied back to back. One of the London papers, the *Perfect Diurnall*, wrote approvingly of Captain Swanley's action and stated that he "made water rats of the papish vermin". Parliament acclaimed his action and presented Captain Swanley with a gold chain worth £200.

When the parliamentarians under Colonel Thomas Mytton captured Shrewsbury in February 1645, they took fifty Irish prisoners. Mytton selected twelve by lot and hanged them in the town square. In retaliation Prince Rupert ordered the hanging of thirteen Roundheads taken at Oswestry. Parliament protested vigorously against this "outrage" and ordered the Earl of Essex to explain to Rupert that "there was a very great difference between Englishmen and Irishmen". Sir William Brereton hanged every Irish prisoner he took, saying that the Irish soldiers "deserved the noose because they were guilty of great spoils and cruelties... horrid rapes and insolencies". Oliver Cromwell concluded that hanging the Irish was "a righteous judgement of God upon these barbarous wretches".

It is not necessary to go too much into the convoluted state of Irish politics before the arrival of Cromwell in Ireland. The Irish were, as usual, divided. Thomas Carlyle, the nineteenth century historian, wrote of them, "Parties on the back of Parties, at war with the world and with each other." In overall command of the royalists was James Butler, twelfth Earl of Ormonde. The Butlers were an old Anglo-Irish Catholic family, but Ormonde was a Protestant, having been made a ward of court and raised in England. In his army, three of his Catholic brothers and several cousins held high commands. Canon O'Rourke in his *The Battle of the Faith in Ireland* (1887) wrote:

> Undoubtedly Ormonde was a man of great parts. His weakest point was, perhaps, the want of high military talents; but as for diplomacy—that is plotting—he was a veritable Palmerston born before his time . . . Ormonde hated the Catholic religion with an intensity which can only belong to a pervert . . . the old Irish whom Ormonde and all Palesmen looked upon as an alien and inferior race, unfit for the same rights and priviledges as Englishmen. . .

Under him served Murrough O'Brien, Lord Inchiquin. He had a varied career: in early life he was a soldier of fortune, serving in the Spanish army in Italy. He was appointed vice-president of Munster by Charles I. When the rebellion of 1641 broke out, he became the scourge of rebels in Munster, sacking and burning, killing and hanging. On the refusal of the king to grant him the presidency of Munster, he joined the parliamentary army and for some years devoted all his energies and military skill to securing that province for the parliamentarians. Inchiquin was responsible for the sacking of Cashel in which he and his men slaughtered the defenders, although he had previously promised them quarter. A short time later he again changed sides, but was not as active on behalf of the king as he had been for the parliamentarians. Because he was a turncoat so many times, he was never really trusted by the Irish; in fact, he was still remembered for his fierce and unrelenting hatred of the Catholic Church. He was known to the Irish as "Murrough the burner". His army was mainly made up of Protestants of English origin.

The Catholic Confederation of Kilkenny, which was set up in 1643, also had a standing army. The pope sent Cardinal Giovanni Battista Rinuccini as papal nuncio to the Confederation in 1645. He was warmly welcomed by some of the officers of the Confederation, including Richard Butler, the brother of the Earl of Ormonde. Rinuccini reported: "At the time of my arrival the greater part of the Catholic troops were under the command of two generals, Owen O'Neill and Thomas Preston, . . . who were not only rivals by nature, and from party spirit, but embittered by jealousy from having both served in the Flemish wars, and from having even then shown signs of mutual aversion."

Owen Roe O'Neill was a scion of the great Clan O'Neill, one of his forebears being Niall of the Nine Hostages who had raided Gaul for slaves. O'Neill, although born in Ireland, was taken to Spain as a child and entered the Spanish army in his youth. He was transferred to the Netherlands in the Spanish service in 1625 and was regarded as one of their ablest commanders there. He returned to Ireland in 1642, assumed command of his northern clansmen and fought the English troops who were devastating the country after the rebellion of 1641.

Ormonde strove to bring O'Neill over to the royalist side, pointing out that now peace had been made between himself and the Catholic Confederation, they should all unite against the common enemy—the parliamentarians. O'Neill hesitated and was proclaimed by the Confederation "a traitor and a rebel". He wrote to Cardinal Rinuccini: "We are almost reduced to despair. On the one hand Ormonde entreats us to join him; on the other, the Parliamentary party seeks our friendship. God knows we hate and detest both alike!"

O'Neill's hatred of Ormonde was such that he eventually joined the parliamentary forcers, under General Monck (or Monk, as it was sometimes spelled). The general gave certain assurances to him, granting him and his men indemnity for the past and assurances that their religion and estates would be respected. O'Neill also received thirty barrels of powder with matches and bullets, 300 cows and £400 in cash, all on condition that he should march to the relief of Derry, then besieged by royalists. O'Neill joined "Butcher" Coote's parliamentary army to lift the siege, but the royalists withdrew on his approach. Sir Charles Coote was the other commander of the parliamentary forces in Ireland, and his father was notorious for his atrocities towards the Irish rebels of 1641. It is all the more surprising, therefore, that Owen Roe O'Neill was prepared to enter an alliance with such a man. The alliance between O'Neill and the parliamentarians did not last long. Monck was recalled from Ireland and imprisoned in the Tower for entering into this alliance with O'Neill; Coote escaped with a reprimand. The arrival of Cromwell forced O'Neill and Ormonde to join forces, but it was too late to have any effect on the campaign there.

On 17 January 1649 a peace was concluded between Ormonde, acting on behalf of Charles I, and the General Assembly of the Confederation. A few days after the signing of this treaty, the news of the king's execution reached Ireland. Ormonde had the Prince of Wales proclaimed king under the title of Charles II. Almost the whole of Ireland supported this move, and for a time the leaders of the various parties forgot their differences.

There were two parliamentary armies in Ireland at the time under the overall command of General Charles Coote, whose father, also a general, was killed by Irish rebels in Trim in 1642. General Monck commanded the other parliamentary army. He was an old campaigner who had fought in most of the battles of the Civil War in England.

There is no doubt, with hindsight, that Ormonde was unfitted for the overall command of the royalist armies. On seeing a portrait of him, Cromwell is reported to have remarked that he looked more like a country gentleman than a soldier. Ormonde had a tendency to blame all his defeats in the field on others, especially the Irish.

The first battle of the parliamentary war in Ireland was fought and won before Cromwell ever reached the country. It took place near Rathmines, County Dublin, on 22 July 1649, between a royalist force of 7000 men under the command of Lieutenant General Ormonde and a much smaller force of 2000 parliamentarians commanded by Colonel Michael Jones. Jones surprised the royalists, who were preparing to besiege Dublin, and in the space of a couple of hours routed them. Ormonde claimed that he lost 600 men, although according to Dr Bate 3000 were slain and 2100 soldiers and 150 officers were taken prisoner, including one of Ormonde's Catholic brothers, Colonel Richard Butler. In addition, the parliamentarians took all their baggage, arms and ammunition, and a money chest containing £4000. Ormonde himself narrowly escaped capture.

As happened in many battles later, he sought to lay the onus on the Irish. In a letter to Charles II he wrote: "It was the right wing of our army; and it was not long before I saw it wholly defeated, and many of them running away towards the hills of Wicklow, where some of them were bred and whither they knew the way but too well."

Cromwell was already on board a ship called the *John* when he received news of Jones' victory. He wrote: "This is an astonishing mercy; so great and seasonable as indeed we are like them that dreamed. What can we say? The Lord fill our souls with thankfulness, that our mouths may be full of his praise."

He sailed from Milford Haven for Ireland on 13 August 1649 with the dual objects of revenging the massacres of 1641 and of bringing Ireland under the Commonwealth. He had with him a fleet of thirty-two ships, while his son-in-law, Commissary General Henry Ireton, followed two days later with the main body of the army in forty-two vessels; and Cromwell's chaplain, Hugh Peters, with another twenty ships, brought up the rear. In all the parliamentary army numbered 20,000 men. They were all trained soldiers, well equipped with an abundant supply of military stores, and more important still, with four big siege guns which could batter the walls of the most heavily fortified towns. He also brought with him an immense store of Bibles and, lastly, a quantity of scythes to cut down the crops which would provide sustenance to the Irish.

After Ormonde's defeat at Rathmines, he arranged a meeting with Owen Roe O'Neill to combine forces to defeat Cromwell. O'Neill sent 3000 men to Ormonde's aid and promised to meet him in the middle of December. The meeting never took place. O'Neill died on 6 November 1649, after a lingering illness. It was rumoured at the time that he had been poisoned by a thorn placed in a pair of russet boots sent to him by an acquaintance named Plunkett.

Cromwell did not waste much time after landing in Dublin; after two days he set out for Drogheda and Dundalk, vital keys to the north. As an old campaigner he knew the value of time and was determined not to allow Ormonde to regroup his scattered army. On 31 August he marched out of the city at the head of 10,000 horse and foot soldiers, with a plentiful supply of provisions and an artillery train such as had not been seen previously in Ireland. Before leaving he issued a proclamation that farmers and other folk who brought provisions to the army were to receive ready money for their goods and not to be troubled or molested in any way. It was a shrewd psychological move on his part; previously the country people had been at the mercy of rapacious, plundering armies who took their provisions without any payment. As an example that the proclamation meant what it said, Cromwell hanged two of his private soldiers for stealing a hen from a countrywoman.

The royalists were resolved to hold Drogheda, and Ormonde ordered the fortifications to be repaired. However, despite the feverish preparations, Drogheda was still short of provisions for a prolonged siege. There was not enough time to prepare the fortifications, which in some cases were still very weak. A week before Cromwell appeared before the city, the governor, Sir Arthur Aston, wrote to Ormonde: "Yesternight there came from Dundalk ten barrels of powder, but very little match; and that is a thing most wanting here; and for round shot, not any at all. I beseech your Excellency to be pleased to give speedy orders for same, as also for the sudden coming of men and moneys. Bellyfood, I perceive will prove scarce amongst us." Ormonde was in no position to send these supplies as his own resources were running low.

The town was held by 2220 foot and 320 horse, nearly all of whom were Irish. They were commanded by Sir Arthur Aston, a Catholic from Cheshire, an old soldier who had served in the army of Poland against the Turks. He had returned to England at the outbreak of the Civil War and was appointed colonel general of dragoons. He saw service at Edgehill, and it was said of him that there was none in the king's army with a greater reputation for bravery. Both he and Ormonde hoped to hold Drogheda until winter set in and hunger and sickness would weaken the besieging forces sufficiently for Ormonde to attack them.

Before the debacle at Rathmines, Ormonde had sent Inchiquin with a force of 2000 men south to Munster after the receipt of a rumour that Cromwell intended to land there. It was only one of the many mistakes of Ormonde's campaign in Ireland. Most of Inchiquin's men were Protestants of English descent and had no wish to fight their fellow countrymen in Cromwell's army. They deserted in squadrons to join the parliamentary army whenever the opportunity offered.

Having encamped his army around the city and placed his batteries of big guns in position, Cromwell on 10 September 1649 sent a demand for surrender to Aston:

> Sir—Having brought the army belonging to the Parliament of England before this place, to reduce it to obedience, to the end effusion of blood may be prevented, I thought fit to summons you to deliver

the same into my hands to their use. If this be refused, you will have no cause to blame me. I expect your answer, and rest your servant,

O. Cromwell

Cromwell's offer was refused. Cromwell lowered the white flag and ran up the red ensign. Later, in a letter to the speaker of Parliament, William Lenthell, he gave a vivid account of the storming of Drogheda:

Upon Tuesday, the 10th of this instant, about five o'clock in the evening, we began the storm; and after some hot dispute we entered, about seven or eight hundred men, the enemy disputing it very stiffly with us. And indeed, through the advantages of the place and the courage God was pleased to give the defenders, our men were forced to retreat, quite out of breath, not without some considerable loss. [Cromwell does not mention that he, sword in hand, led the second assault.] Although our men that stormed the breaches were forced to recoil . . . yet, being encouraged to recover their loss, they made a second attempt, wherein God was pleased so to animate them that they got ground of the enemy, and, by the goodness of God, forced him to quit his entrenchments.

God must have been busy that day in Drogheda. Later that night the Roundheads were the victors and ran amok. No mercy was shown as Cromwell had declared on the previous day that if the defenders of Drogheda held out, no quarter would be given. Ormonde later hotly disputed this: "All the officers and soldiers promised quarter to such as would lay down their arms, and performed it as long as any place held out; which encouraged others to yield. But when they had once all in their power and feared no hurt that could be done them, then the word no quarter went round, and the soldiers were forced, many of them against their wills, to kill the prisoners."

In all, forty-four captains, all lieutenants and ensigns, 220 reformadoes (an officer who for some reason was deprived of his command, but retained his rank) and troopers and 2500 foot soldiers were killed, according to a list published in the *Perfect Diurnall* in London on 2 October 1649. All these had been promised quarter. Others, seeing the fate of their commanders, determined to fight to the bitter end.

According to a report at the time by Cromwell:

> Divers of the officers and soldiers being fled over the bridge into the other part of the town, whereabout a hundred of them possessed St. Peter's church-steeple, some the West gate, others a strong round tower next the gate called St. Sunday's. These being summoned to yield to mercy, refused, wherupon I ordered the steeple of the St. Peter's church to be fired, when one of them was heard to say in the midst of the flames, "God damn me, God confound me, I burn, I burn."

Colonel Michael Jones, the victor of Rathmines, who was second-in-command to Cromwell, told him that now he had the flower of the Irish army in his hands and could deal with them as he pleased. Cromwell then issued an order that the life of neither man, woman nor child should be spared; and when one of his officers pleaded for mercy for the unresisting victims, he said he "would sacrifice their souls to the ghosts of the English whom they had massacred".

Cromwell gave an account of the death of Sir Arthur Aston:

> The enemy retreated divers of them to the Mill Mount: a place very strong and of difficult access, being exceeding high, having a good graft, and strongly palisaded. The Governor, Sir Arthur Aston, and divers considerable officers being there, our men getting up to them, were ordered by me to put them all to the sword. And, indeed, being in the heat of action, I forbade them to spare any that were in arms

in the town; and I think that night they put to the
sword about 2000 men.

Sir Arthur Aston had a wooden leg and the soldiers
believed that he had hidden gold in it; not finding it they
proceeded to bludgeon him with his own wooden stump,
and then hacked his body to pieces. The slaughter went on
all that night and for the next four days. Not only were the
defenders killed in cold blood, but priests and nuns were
especially singled out and slaughtered in a particularly
gruesome manner. A manuscript history of these events,
written at the time by one of the Jesuit Fathers employed
on the Irish mission and preserved in the archives of the
Irish College in Rome, gives some further details of the
cruelty exercised towards the priests that were seized:

> When the city was captured by the heretics, the blood
> of the Catholics was mercilessly shed in the streets, in
> the dwelling-houses, and in the open fields; to none
> was mercy shown; not to the women, not to the aged,
> nor to the young . . . On the following day, when the
> soldiers were searching through the ruins on the city,
> they discovered one of our Fathers, named John
> Bathe [Taaffe], with his brother, a secular priest.
> Suspecting that they were religious, they examined
> them, and finding that they were priests and one of
> them, moreover, a Jesuit, they led them off in tri-
> umph, and accompanied by a tumultuous crowd,
> conducted them to the market-place, and there, as if
> they were at length extinguishing the Catholic reli-
> gion and our Society, they tied them both to stakes
> fixed in the ground and pierced their bodies with
> shots till they expired.

Cromwell, referring to the storming of Drogheda, wrote
in a letter to John Bradshaw, president of the Council of
State, dated 17 September 1649: "It hath pleased God to
bless our endeavours at Drogheda. The enemy were about
3000 strong in the town . . . Before we entered we refused

them quarter; having the day before summoned the town. I do not think Thirty of the whole number escaped with their lives. Those that did are in safe custody for Barbadoes."

Yet in another letter to the speaker of the Parliament in England, also dated on the same day as before, he wrote:

> The next day the two other towers were summoned, in one of which was about six or seven score, but they refused to yield themselves; and we, knowing that hunger must compel them, set only good guards to secure them from running away until their stomachs were come down. From one of the said towers, notwithstanding their condition they killed and wounded some of our men. When they submitted, their officers were knocked on the head and every tenth man of the soldiers killed, and the rest shipped to the Barbadoes. The soldiers in the other tower were all spared (as to their lives only), and shipped likewise for the Barbadoes.

This would show that a greater number were shipped there than Cromwell indicated in his first letter. In the years that followed, many thousands more men, women and children were shipped into slavery to Barbados and the other colonies.

CHAPTER TWO

The Rape of Wexford

"Before God's altar fell sacred victims, holy priests of the Lord. Of those who were seized outside the church some were scourged, some thrown into chains and imprisoned, while others were hanged or put to death by cruel tortures. The blood of our noblest citizens was shed so that it inundated the streets. There was hardly a house that was not defiled with carnage and filled with wailing."
Dr Nicholas French, Bishop of Ferns, writing to the papal nuncio (January 1673)

IMMEDIATELY AFTER THE capture and sack of Drogheda, Cromwell sent a body of his men under Colonel Chidley Coote to Dundalk, which fell without a shot being fired. Another part of his army went to Trim, which had been abandoned by Ormonde in such haste that the stores, ammunition and guns, which Colonel Aston had begged for, were left abandoned.

Cromwell returned to Dublin an acclaimed hero. He left the city within a fortnight, heading south, with the four great guns that had battered Drogheda, 4000 foot soldiers, 1200 horse and 400 dragoons in his train. Castle after castle, strong point after strong point either surrendered to him or the defenders fled at his approach.

On 29 September the parliamentary fleet, under Sir

George Ayscue (or Ascough), reached the harbour of Wexford. They had sailed along the coast to give close support to the parliamentary army on the way south. On 1 October Cromwell's army camped before the walls of the city. Ormonde was determined to hold Wexford, of vital importance to him because it was through it that he obtained supplies of arms and ammunition from the Continent. The townspeople were, as usual, divided in their loyalties. Some of the old Irish, represented by a man named Rochford, a recorder of the town, had already been in correspondence with Cromwell and were anxious to come to terms with him, relying on him more than on Ormonde. To them Lord Inchiquin, who had sent two regiments of horse into the town, was as great an enemy as Cromwell. They remembered his devastation of Munster and his massacre of the defenders of Cashel. It was only when Sir Edmund Butler, another Catholic brother of Ormonde, arrived with his forces that they accepted Lieutenant Colonel David Sinnott as their governor.

On 3 October Cromwell summoned the town to surrender in a letter to Sinnott. The latter replied that he desired to consult the mayor and other officials before giving an answer. While letters were being exchanged between Sinnott and the Lord Protector, the mayor and aldermen sent Cromwell a present of "sack, strong waters and strong beer".

Negotiations for the surrender went on for several days. In the mean time Cromwell sited his big guns so that if negotiations broke down they were in position to batter the castle, the key to the town. Cromwell began to lose patience with what he regarded as the deliberate delaying tactics of Sinnott, and on 11 October his big guns began a cannonade of the castle walls. Within a few hours some breaks were made, and Sinnott sent four of his officers to parley for terms. One of the four chosen was a Captain Stafford, governor of the castle, described by a contemporary as "a vain, idle young man, nothing practiced in the art military". Somehow Cromwell was able to speak with Stafford alone and, playing on the young man's vanity, induced him to surrender the castle. When the parliamentary troops took possession of it, they were able to open the gates, enabling the remainder of their forces to enter. The defenders and the townspeople withdrew to the market place.

Cromwell's soldiers again ran amok in Wexford and their officers seemed incapable of restraining them. Cromwell needed the town for winter quarters, but the soldiers did so much damage to property that the town became uninhabitable. They killed indiscriminately, defenders and civilians alike; priests, monks and nuns were again especially singled out and tortured before being killed. This is borne out in a letter to the papal nuncio written by Dr Nicholas French, the Bishop of Ferns, who was lying ill in a neighbouring town and thus escaped the slaughter: "On that fatal day, October 11th, 1649, I lost everything I had. Wexford, my native town, then abounding in merchandise, ships, and wealth, was taken at the sword's point by that plague of England, Cromwell, and sacked by an infuriated soldiery."

Reverend Denis Murphy, SJ, in *Cromwellian Ireland* (1885), quotes from a contemporary report: "On the 11th October, his Excellency took Wexford by storm, and in it 51 peeces of ordnance, besides those in ships, 40 vessels in the harbour, great store of plunder, 2000 were slaine of Ormonde's soldiers in the town." Cromwell himself wrote to John Bradshaw, president of the Council of State: "I believe in all there was lost of the enemy not many less than two thousand, and I believe not twenty of yours killed, from first to last of the siege."

The defenders obviously just threw down their arms and surrendered. Sir Edmund Butler was shot as he was endeavouring to escape by swimming across the ferry. According to some writers of the period, a massacre of some 300 women took place at a cross in Wexford; every one of them was killed, and rings which they wore were hacked off their fingers. Cromwell and his officers did nothing to stop the slaughter. Because the town was uninhabitable and the place stank of rotting corpses, he decided to pull his army out of Wexford and march on his next objective, and two days later he approached Ross.

His troops were now weary of the campaign and regretted the destruction of Wexford. Cromwell was forced to leave one of his big guns behind; his men, almost in a state of mutiny, had refused to haul it. Ross was defended by a body of the Catholic Confederation army under Sir Lucas Taaffe, a young and inexperienced man. Cromwell sent his usual demand for surrender to avoid "an effusion of blood". Taaffe replied that he was ready to surrender provided that his men were allowed to march out with arms, bag and baggage, if the lives of the citizens were spared and if they were granted "liberty of conscience".

Cromwell immediately replied: "Sir, To what I formerly offered, I shall make good. . . For that which you mention concerning liberty of conscience, I meddle not with any man's conscience. But if by liberty of conscience you mean a liberty to exercise the Mass, I judge it best to use plain dealing, and to let you know, where the Parliament of England have power, that will not be allowed of." At the same time he placed his three big guns and gave orders to open fire on the walls. After only three shots Taaffe surrendered. Cromwell, in an unexpected show of magnanimity, allowed the defenders to march out of the town, with "arms, bag and baggage, and with drums and colours". Five hundred English soldiers of Inchiquin's regiment, who were among the defenders, went over to the parliamentary side; the remaining 1500 went with Taaffe to Kilkenny. This was yet another blow to Ormonde's plan of campaign, as he had expected Ross to hold out for some considerable time.

Cromwell intended to use Ross as winter quarters but his plans were changed by a singular stroke of good fortune:

the garrison of Cork revolted. Under the command of Lord Broghill, a son of Richard Boyle, first Earl of Cork, it declared for Parliament and drove the Irish inhabitants out of the city. Other towns in Munster also followed suit: Youghal, Bandon, Baltimore, Mallow, Cappoquin and Dungarvan. The royalists lost some of the best-fortified centres in this revolt, which caused a further split between the Protestants under Ormonde and Inchiquin and the soldiers of the Catholic Confederacy.

Illness prevented Cromwell from marching to Cork immediately. He remained in Ross "very sick and crazy" in his health. Writing to William Lenthall he confided that "a considerable part of your army is fitter for the hospital than the field", and added a significant point: "if the enemy did not know it I should have held it impolitic to have writ it. They know it, yet they know not what to do."

At this time Ormonde had an army of 13,000 men and 4000 horse, and was further strengthened by the arrival of Hugh O'Neill, Owen Roe's nephew, with a force of 1500 foot and 500 horse. They made one stipulation on joining Ormonde: that they should fight by themselves, a further proof of the disunity in Ormonde's camp.

Cromwell left Ross on 21 November, apparently fully recovered from his illness, but leaving some of his sick men behind. Ormonde estimated that the parliamentary army had only an effective fighting force of some 4000 foot, 2000 horse and 500 dragoons. Despite the superiority of his own army, he made no attempt to engage them in battle and allowed them to march unhindered on Waterford, Cromwell's last objective before going into winter quarters.

The parliamentarians anticipated that the city would surrender without a fight, having in mind the fate of Drogheda and Wexford. Indeed, the mayor and certain wealthy citizens wanted to surrender immediately, but the governor, Lieutenant General Richard Ferrall, who had much experience of sieges in Flanders, was made of sterner stuff. He had

2000 Ulstermen with him in the city, which was protected with strong defences and heavy, well-sited artillery. He returned an uncompromising rejection to Cromwell's demand for surrender. Cromwell, realising that a long siege would be impossible in winter, wisely decided to withdraw. The weather had turned foul, and the ground became so muddy that it would not bear the weight of his siege guns. During the short time the siege lasted 1000 men died of malaria and dysentery. Because of the state of the ground and the weakness of the remainder of his army, he was forced to abandon his remaining three heavy guns.

On 2 December Cromwell began a march towards Dungarvan. "It being," he wrote, "so terrible a day as ever I marched in my life." He lost over 1000 men on this march, including one of his senior officers, Colonel Horton, and his own cousin, also called Oliver. Cromwell, commenting on his losses in a letter to Lenthall, wrote: "Thus you see how God mingles out the cup to us." Parliamentarians refused the services of Catholic doctors because they were convinced that they would poison them. "Our condition," one wrote, "for want of physicians is sad, being fain to trust our lives in the Popish doctors' hands, when we fall sick, which is much, if not more than our adventures in the field." This sentiment appeared in a letter in the *Perfect Diurnall*, 8 January 1650. Colonel Michael Jones, the man who defeated Ormonde at Rathmines, died in Dungarvan, probably of malaria. A rumour swept the army that Cromwell had poisoned him out of jealousy, although two days later, he gave the funeral oration at Jones' burial. In Youghal Cromwell met up with Lord Broghill with some 2500 men of the southern garrisons that had recently gone over to Parliament.

The army remained in Youghal until the end of January, enjoying a well-earned rest. Recruits, medicines and provisions poured in from England. But the sojourn was no idle rest for Cromwell; he made a tour of almost all the cities and towns that had gone over to the parliamentary cause.

His first visit was to Cork, accompanied by Lord Broghill, and here, according to Thomas Herbert, clerk of the Council, "His Excellency was received with very hearty and noble entertainment." At Kinsale the mayor came out and delivered to him the town mace and keys of the gates. Instead of returning them to the mayor, he handed them over to Colonel Stubber, whom he appointed as governor of the town. He said that he had been told that the mayor was an Irishman and a Papist, and that he judged it inconvenient to entrust a place of such importance to one of that creed. When later he was told that Stubber was not overscrupulous in his religious duties, Cromwell is purported to have replied: "May be not, but as he is a soldier he has honour, and therefore we will let his religion alone this time."

It was while in winter quarters in Youghal that Cromwell received what became known as the Clonmacnoise Decrees. The bishops and leading clergy of Ireland, twenty-five in all, assembled there on 4 December 1649, and declared:

> [W]e do hereby declare as a most certain truth that the enemy's resolution is to extirpate the Catholic religion . . . and it is notoriously known that by the Acts of Parliament called the Acts of Subscription the estates of the inhabitants of this Kingdom are sold so that there remaineth now no more but to put the purchasers in possession by the power of forces drawn out of England. And for the common sort of people . . . intending at the close of their conquest (if they can effect the same, as (God forbid) to root out the commons also, and plant this land with colonies to be brought hither out of England, as witness the number they have already sent hence for the Tobacco Island and put enemies in their place.

The "Tobacco Island" was, of course, Barbados.

Cromwell issued a blistering reply to the Decrees. He

wrote it in Youghal and it was first printed in Cork and reprinted in London in March 1650:

> Here is your argument: The design is to extirpate the Catholic Religion; but this is not to be done but by the massacring, banishing, or otherwise destroying the Catholic Inhabitants: . . .
>
> Well, your words are, "Massacre, destroy, and banish." Good now. Give us an instance of one man since my coming into Ireland, not in arms, massacred, destroyed, or banished; concerning the massacre or the destruction of whom justice hath not been done, or endeavoured to be done. And as for the other banishment, I must now speak unto the People, whom you would delude, and whom this most concerns; that they may know in this also what to expect at my hands.
>
> The question is of the destruction of life; or of that which is little inferior to it, to wit, of banishment . . . it hath not hitherto been inflicted upon any but such who, being in arms, might justly, upon the terms they were taken, have been put to death; as those who are instanced in your Declaration to be "sent to the Tobacco Islands" . . .
>
> For such of the Nobility, Gentry, and Commons of Ireland, as have not been actors in this Rebellion, they shall and may expect the protection of their Goods, Liberties, and Lives . . .

Cromwell seems to have forgotten in this reply the innocent men, women and children who were massacred at Drogheda and Wexford. The bishops mentioned "the number they have already sent hence for the Tobacco Island", but they could not have foreseen that in the following decade 50,000 innocent people would be sent there as slave labour by the man who admitted it was little inferior to a destruction of life. As for "the Nobility, Gentry, and Commons of Ireland", instead of being left to enjoy their

"Goods, Liberties, and Lives", they were uprooted and forcibly transplanted to the poorest province of Ireland—Connaught.

By 29 January 1650, Cromwell's parliamentary army was ready and eager to take the field.

Cromwell, in a letter from Cork on 20 January, wrote: "The army is in good health, that regiments which lately had marched only 400 men, now march 800 or 900."

Only five major cities now remained in the hands of the royalists: Waterford, Clonmel, Limerick, Galway and Kilkenny. Cromwell's next objective was Kilkenny, the headquarters of the Catholic Confederacy. Ormonde had made it his winter headquarters and had taken the opportunity to fortify it. He left it at the beginning of January to recruit more men and to replenish his dwindling stores of arms and ammunition. Again he found dissension in the ranks of the Irish army. Lord Dillon, with 2500 foot, refused his orders to remain and hold the city and with his men marched north.

At Kilkenny Cromwell issued his usual demand for its surrender. The governor, Walter Butler, another Catholic brother of Ormonde, refused, but the mayor, unbeknown to the governor, established a communication with Cromwell, and on 28 March the city and castle were given up on condition that the city paid 2000 pounds as a gratuity to the parliamentary army.

Cromwell did not remain long in Kilkenny where a plague was raging, but marched on Clonmel, which was held by Hugh O'Neill with a force of 1500 men. As usual Cromwell called for the surrender of the town, but was met with a blank refusal. Cromwell set up his remaining artillery pieces and battered the walls, eventually making a breach. O'Neill had erected inner defences of timber and stone and sited his guns so that they could sweep the parliamentary ranks as they advanced through the breach. At eight o'clock on the morning of 27 April, the parliamentarians rushed in, and as they did so the Irish guns opened up on them. Within an hour they had lost over 1000 men. Cromwell, waiting outside the gates, saw the few survivors retreating through the breach and "was much vexed as ever he was since he first put on a helmet against the King, for such a repulse he did not usually meet with". As foot soldiers refused to advance a second time, Cromwell called up his cavalry, under the command of his best officers. They rode through the breach, but, like the infantry, were also devastated by O'Neill's cleverly sited guns and retreated leaving 2000 of their number dead within the town.

Cromwell was on the point of raising the siege when a regiment of foot and 300 horse reached him and to save face he decided to remain and starve out the defenders. The siege lasted two months until eventually O'Neill, whose ammunition was nearly spent and whose provisions were so low that the townspeople were eating dogs and cats, decided to withdraw. He did so at night, passing unnoticed through a gap in the besiegers' ranks. Next morning the mayor surrendered the town to Cromwell who, admiring the bravery of the defenders, refused to sanction a slaughter of the inhabitants.

Clonmel was Cromwell's last military action in Ireland. He was recalled by Parliament, and on the 29 May set sail from Youghal in a new frigate. He had been in Ireland for just over nine months, and in that time had reduced a country to submission. Nobody can ever question his bravery, and in England he received a hero's welcome; but in Ireland "the Curse of Cromwell" is still used as a malediction.

In summing up Cromwell's campaign in Ireland, it is well to note one of the apologies made on Cromwell's behalf by John Buchan. Writing in his book *Cromwell* (1970), he makes this point:

> [F]irst we must note a physical fact. He was in bad health. Before Christmas he had an actual breakdown, some form of malaria which was the country

epidemic, but from the start his bodily condition was abnormal. It had been so ever since the difficult days before the second Civil War, and it was to continue so, with interludes of serious illness, till after Worcester. He took a doctor with him, a step which in the old days he would have scorned. The balance of his nature was maladjusted; mind preyed upon body, and body distempered mind.

However nothing can excuse Cromwell's extreme cruelty in Ireland. No matter what his medical condition, the savagery at Drogheda shocked even his most faithful followers. Even some of his commanders, including old campaigners like Ludlow, thought the slaughter at Drogheda "extraordinary". Cromwell admitted in a letter to Lenthall that he personally had led the charge on Mill Mount, although quarter had already been given and revoked by himself at the last minute. He also ordered the firing of St Peter's Church steeple in which one hundred people were sheltering. His excuse for all this bloodletting was to instil terror and thus save lives. "The enemy were filled with much terror. And truly I believe this bitterness will save much blood through the goodness of God." Another reason he gave for the savagery at Drogheda was that it was a "righteous judgement of God upon these barbarous wretches, who have imbrued their hands in so much innocent blood". Cromwell's third excuse for the slaying of the garrison was that it was the law of war. If the defenders of a fortress which had been summoned to surrender had refused, they then had no claim to mercy, the more so if the fortress was patently indefensible.

Of Drogheda, Buchan writes:

> In Ireland he was false to his own creed. Never in the English wars, except at Basing, had he been anything but merciful. He knew that he had erred and therefore he tried to justify his conduct to Lenthall, a thing, it may fairly be said, that no other soldier of

the day would have dreamed of. His confusion of spirit is shown by his excuse of a heat of temper, which in his sober moments he would have held to be a sin. It is shown by his childish tale of the blasphemy of some poor creature in the agony of burning, as if that justified the enormity. He is trying to batter his soul into complacence.

On the other hand, the chivalry he had displayed at Marston Moor and Naseby sometimes returned. For instance, he allowed the garrison of Fethard, County Tipperary, to surrender and to march out of the town with full military honours. The articles of surrender read as follows:

> That all the officers and soldiers shall march freely with their horses and arms and all other goods, bag and baggage, colours flying, matches lighted...
>
> That all the country families and inhabitants, as also any of the officers may freely live and enjoy their goods either in town or abroad.

The third article is even more extraordinary:

> That all clergymen and captains of soldiers, both town and country now in this garrison, may freely march bag and baggage without any annoyance of prejudice in body or goods.

These articles of surrender were signed by Oliver Cromwell himself.

Cromwell, when accepting the surrender of Kilkenny, praised their garrison under the command of Walter Butler (Ormonde's brother) for their courage in defence of that city, and also allowed the garrison to march out with bag and baggage and with colours flying.

Perhaps Cromwell's character is best summed up in Thomas Carlyle's words: "Armed Soldier, terrible as Death, relentless as Doom; doing God's judgement on the Enemies of God. It is a phenomenon not of joyful nature; no, but of awful, to be looked at with pious terror and awe."

CHAPTER THREE

Transplantation

"To hell or to Connaught"
Saying attributed to Cromwell

CROMWELL'S DEPARTURE DID not end the war in Ireland; Limerick, Waterford and Galway still held out. Waterford surrendered on reasonable terms to Ireton, whom Cromwell had appointed as governor on his departure. Ireton then laid siege to Limerick. Hugh O'Neill, the hero of Clonmel, was governor, and he refused all Ireton's terms of surrender. The city held out for a year, but again starvation and lack of ammunition forced O'Neill to make terms. Plague also raged in the city, and thousands died from it. Ireton was so impressed with O'Neill's bravery and soldierly qualities that he gave special orders that his life was to be spared, although many of Ireton's senior officers wanted him killed in retaliation for his defence of Clonmel. It is an ironic fact of history that Ireton died of the plague a few days after the surrender of Limerick, and that when his body was shipped back to England for a state funeral, O'Neill should be on the same ship, bound for imprisonment in the Tower. Before he died, Ireton's last act was to write a letter to Parliament requesting them to "use the brave warrior with all civility and humanity". O'Neill spent some months in the Tower, but on an appeal by the Spanish ambassador he was allowed to go to Spain, where he entered the Spanish service.

Galway fell soon afterwards; the city had also been stricken by the plague. Sir Charles Coote, known as "the Butcher of Connaught", did not behave as magnanimously as did Ireton, and ordered most of the leaders to be executed.

There was now only one Irish army in the field: the Ulstermen, which still numbered some 5000 foot and 600 horse. On Owen Roe O'Neill's death there had been a dispute for the leadership: Owen Roe's son, Henry, was considered to be too young and inexperienced; Daniel O'Neill, Owen Roe's nephew, should have been chosen as he had seen service with the Spaniards in the Netherlands, but he was a Protestant. Finally Heber MacMahon, a bishop, was chosen. It was the worst possible choice that could have been made. He was summed up by a contemporary as follows: "As for the bishop, though a good politician, he was no more a soldier fit to be a general than one of Rome's cardinals." He was certainly no strategist: a short time after his appointment, he risked taking on a parliamentary force under Generals Coote and Venables against the advice of Daniel O'Neill and the other senior officers. On 21 June 1652 the battle of Scariffhollis began, and by nightfall the Irish army was routed. No quarter was given, and over 3000 were killed. Those taken prisoner were hanged the following day; all the leaders were beheaded. The bishop, although wounded, escaped, but was captured a few days later and hanged, drawn and quartered; his head was placed on a pike over the walls of Derry.

Shortly after the defeat at Scariffhollis, Ormonde, whose final mistake in Ireland was to confirm the appointment of Bishop MacMahon as commander of the Irish army of Ulster, left for Paris, where he joined the court in exile of Charles II. Of him Cardinal Rinuccini, the papal nuncio, wrote as early as 1646, that all the "broils" arose from one source alone, the faction of the Marquis of Ormonde. At the Restoration he returned to England with King Charles II, was again appointed lord lieutenant of Ireland, and died in 1688, aged seventy-seven.

Lord Inchiquin also went to France to join Charles, and also returned with him to England. He, too, was restored to his estate and was granted a sum of £8000 for the losses he had sustained. He never returned to Ireland for fear of assassination by both sides, considering his past actions. In a last volte-face he became a Catholic and in the remaining years of his life performed many good works. He died in 1674, and in his will left £20 to the Franciscan monastery of Ennis, and also a large sum of money "for the performance of the usual duties of the Roman Catholic clergy and for other pious uses".

One question still remained to be resolved by Parliament: what to do with the 34,000 (some historians put the figure as high as 40,000) Irish prisoners of war held in gaols and camps throughout Ireland. Their upkeep, such as it was, had become a strain on the Exchequer. Cromwell's solution to send them as slaves to Barbados was unworkable. It would have been feasible to send the thirty or so he had captured in Drogheda, or even 300, but if 34,000 or 40,000 were sent they would have outnumbered the planters two to one. Parliament finally decided to allow the men to go to any country of their choice not at war with England: France, Spain, Austria and Poland.

There was certainly a demand for these Irish soldiers abroad. Irishmen had been fighting in the various armies of Europe from the time of Queen Elizabeth I. Irish regiments served in the Low Countries, and many who had seen service in the Seven Years War returned to Ireland to fight the parliamentarians there. The Prince of Orange declared that they were born soldiers. Henry IV of France called Hugh O'Neill, the defender of Clonmel and Limerick, the third soldier of his age, and stated that no nation produced better troops than the Irish if they were properly drilled and led. Even an Englishman, Sir John Norris, praised their valour and said that he knew no nation where there were so few fools or cowards.

Recruiting agents from many countries flocked to Ireland to enlist their services. Don Ricardo White, in May 1652, shipped 7000 men from the ports of Waterford, Kinsale, Galway, Limerick and Bantry for service in the Spanish army. In the following September, Colonel Christopher Mayo sent another batch of 3000 to serve the Spanish king. Sir Walter Dugan got permission to march prisoners of war to various ports, with pipes playing at the head of each column, to embark for Spain. Lord Muskerry took 5000 soldiers to Poland to serve the king there. He received special permission from Parliament to do so, and it also declared that while they were awaiting shipment they were not to be transplanted. Other prisoners of war left in smaller batches to enlist in the armies of France and Austria. There was one great snag in the seeming altruism of Parliament: soldiers were not allowed to take their dependants abroad with them.

With the departure of the soldiers, Ireland was, as one English historian put it, like "a blank sheet of paper". An act was quickly passed in the English Parliament in 1652, quaintly named the Act of Good Affection. It classified Irish and Anglo-Irish Catholics and Protestants under different qualifications of guilt. The first dealt with Irish chiefs, nobility, or indeed anybody who was alleged to have taken part in the rebellion of 1641. They were sentenced to death, and 200 of them, including Sir Phelim O'Neill, were hanged in Kilkenny in 1652. All their property in Ulster was confiscated. The second classification of guilt referred to the Irish and Anglo-Irish who fought against Cromwell. They were either sentenced to death or to banishment, and their lands were also forfeited to the government. The last clause in the act was all embracing: it stated that all Irish Catholics who had taken no part in the war of 1649–52, but had "remained quiet", were again liable to be transplanted, unless they had "manifested a constant good affection in favour of Parliament and against the King". This act applied to almost the whole population of Ireland, as Dublin and Derry were the only cities held by the parliamentarians when Cromwell landed. The decision for the wholesale clearance of the land was made by Cromwell and the Council of State on 2 July 1653 and confirmed by an act of Parliament on 26 September.

It was by far the most draconian plan ever devised for the complete ethnic cleansing of Ireland. The richest provinces of Munster, Leinster and Ulster were set aside to be planted by English settlers, while the poorest and most infertile province, Connaught, was to be reserved for the Irish, who were forced to transplant there. Connaught had been ravaged by Sir Charles Coote and his parliamentary army. His father has gone down in history as the man who ordered his troops, when quelling the rebellion of 1641, to kill every man and women, and every child "more than a span long". When some of his officers objected to the killing of infants, Coote is purported to have replied, "Kill the nits and you will have no lice."

Even all of Connaught was not to be given over to those transplanted. One of the few fertile counties in that province, Mayo, was deleted from the area allowed to the people transplanted, as were two of the richest baronies in Galway and Clare. Henry, Cromwell's son, was given Portumna Castle, park and gardens along with 6000 acres; Sir Charles Coote was rewarded with extensive lands in Clare.

The richest towns and cities of the three provinces, including Cork and Dublin, were reserved for the government in settlement of its own debts. Other portions of the country were allocated to meet the arrears of pay of the soldiers of the parliamentary army who at that time were owed over £1,500,000. The remainder of the land was set aside to satisfy the Adventurers, a body set up in 1641, which loaned Parliament a sum of money and hoped to receive Irish lands in settlement, who were now owed over £360,000.

This act also ordered that all transplantation of the Irish was to be completed by 1 May 1654. Those who had not transplanted by that date were to be hanged. A commission was set up in Loughrea, County Galway, to examine all those transplanted and to allocate lands in Connaught to them. They were given roughly 10 per cent of their former estates. Heads of transplanted families, with their wives, children and some of their servants, had to travel, very often on foot and in the depth of winter, to reach Loughrea before that deadline. They were allowed to bring their cattle and grain with them, but owing to the condition of the roads and the lack of transport, this was often impossible. It is believed that as many people died in that terrible exodus as were killed during the war itself.

Many of the Irish nobility, gentry and leading proprietors had taken no part in the war, but this did not save them from transplantation, because their properties were required for the new English planters. Ploughmen, labourers and most of the working classes were excepted from transplantation. John P. Prendergast's *The Cromwellian Settlement of Ireland* (1996) includes an anecdote told by a monk of the order of the Friars Minor, who had lived disguised as a servant in the household of Colonel Ingoldesby, governor of Limerick, that explains why the common people were allowed to stay and the gentry were required to transplant. He heard a Cromwellian statesman giving three reasons for it: "First," the statesman said, "they were useful to the English as earth-tillers and herdsmen; secondly, deprived of their priests and gentry, and living among the English, it is hoped they would become Protestants; and thirdly, the gentry, without their aid, must work for themselves and their families and so, in time, turn into common peasants or die if they don't."

This policy of transplanting only the heads of families and their close relatives was opposed very strongly by the officers who had been given their lands, in a document entitled "The humble Petition of the Officers within the Precincts of Dublin, Carlow, Wexford, and Kilkenny, in the behalf of themselves, their Souldiers, and other faithful English Protestants, to the Lord Deputy and Council of Ireland." They pray that the original order of the Council of State in England, confirmed by Parliament, 27 September 1653, requiring the removal of all the Irish nation into Connaught, except boys of fourteen and girls of twelve, might be enforced:

> For we humbly conceive, that the proclamation for transplanting only the proprietors and such as have bin in arms will neither answer the end of safety nor what else is aimed at thereby. For the purpose of the transplantation is to prevent those of natural principles [i.e., of natural affections] becoming one with these Irish, as well in affinity as idolatry, as many thousands did, who came over in Queen Elizabeth's time, many of which have had a deep hand in all the late murthers and massacres. And shall we join in affinity with the people of these abominations?

However, not all the officers and soldiers wanted to stay in Ireland and take up the land allotted to them. Some were homesick, others were reluctant to become farmers or were unable or unwilling to supply the capital required to purchase cattle or to build a house. Some complained that the land allotted to them was boggy and unfit for cultivation; others simply sold their allotments to their senior officers or gambled them away in card games. Thus we find that vast estates were obtained by senior officers' buying up soldiers' land.

Some people tried to appeal against the order for transplantation, but in vain. For instance, Maurice, Viscount Roche of Castletownroche in County Cork, spent £600 in travelling to Dublin to appeal personally to the Lords of the Council. His plea was turned down. He then appealed to Cromwell and received no response. Lady Roche had defended her castle on Cromwell's march south, and because he had no heavy guns he could not take it. However, after his stay in winter quarters, he sent a detachment of the army to take Castletownroche, this time with heavy artillery. Lady Roche again defended the castle for several days until Cromwell's guns battered it into submission. She was kept a prisoner in Cork for four years and then tried, found guilty (being falsely accused by an English maidservant of shooting a man) and hanged. Maurice Roche was turned out of the castle with his four daughters and was not allowed to carry any provisions with him. He was forced to travel on foot from Castletownroche to Loughrea in the middle of winter, depending on the charity of people through whose lands he passed. One of his daughters died of malnutrition on the way. The Commissioners awarded him 2500 acres of barren land (his family had owned 24,000 acres of prime land in Cork); and to compound his sufferings, he was later evicted from this land in Connaught, the commissioners having, through an oversight, awarded it to somebody else. He died soon afterwards, and his daughters were forced to become needlewomen to subsist.

Cromwell behaved in an entirely different manner when an appeal against transplantation was made to him by William Spenser of Kilcolman, County Cork. Spenser was the grandson of the Elizabethan poet Edmund Spenser, who had been granted tracts of land near Doneraile, a few miles from Castletownroche. Cromwell wrote to the Commissioners for Affairs in Ireland pleading William Spenser's case. He pointed out that Spenser was only seven years old at the time of the 1641 rebellion and that his father and grandfather were both Protestants. William had become a Catholic at one stage, but had "since his coming to years of discretion . . . utterly renounced" that religion. Nonetheless, Cromwell's appeal did not save William Spenser from transplantation. His lands had already been taken over by a high ranking parliamentarian officer, and the commissioners must have felt that it was not politic to dispossess him of them.

Meanwhile, the transplantations went on apace. The five commissioners at Loughrea were kept busy processing all the applications. Colonel Donogh O'Callaghan, chief of the Clan O'Callaghan, was one of the first to be transplanted. He was one of the members of the Catholic Confederacy and was lucky to have escaped with his life. He arrived at Loughrea in May 1653 with "a young wife, twenty servants, two nags and thirty beeves [cattle], and with fifty bags of seed corn". He was allocated 2700 acres in Clare, at a place later known as O'Callaghan's Mills, where a branch of the family still live.

Neither sickness nor old age was accepted as an excuse for not transplanting. Sir Nicholas Comyn of Limerick, "who was numb on one side of his body of a dead palsy", as the certificate described him, was still forced to go, accompanied only by his wife, Catherine Comyn, and one maid, to be given 1500 acres in a barren part of Clare.

Widows and orphans were not exempt either. Catherine Morris, a widow of Lackagh, County Limerick, took with her ten cows, ten horses, nineteen goats, two swine and twenty bags of corn, and was allocated 2400 acres in Galway. Ignatious Stackpool, also of Limerick, aged eleven, and Catherine Stackpool, aged eight, orphans, were also transplanted. Records do not show what became of them.

However, certain exceptions were made. Irish widows of the nobility and "ancient English gentry", ladies such as Viscountess Mayo, Lady Grace Talbot, Lady Dunboyne and others were given good lands in Athlone in Galway, and Tulla and Bunratty in Clare, but like all the Irish they received only 10 per cent of their former estates. One old lady, however, the Lady Dowager of Louth, because of her "great age and impotence", was "dispensed with from transplantation".

Another curious case was that of a Mrs Elinor Butler, who was transplanted to Connaught and then, on an appeal, was allowed to return to her own property. She petitioned the commissioners at Loughrea for the return of her cattle, which were still in Connaught. The petition was granted on the recommendation of Colonel Lawrence, one of the commissioners. She must have been one of the very few, who being transplanted, not only received permission for herself and her children to return, but was also given permission for her cattle to be returned to her. The order was dated in Dublin, October 1656, and signed by Thomas Herbert, clerk of the Council.

Protestants were not exempt from transplantation. A Mrs Mary Thorpe, otherwise Dillon, was a Protestant married to a Catholic, and while she and her husband were transplanted, she was given special privileges because she was "a person fearing God and affecting His worship and ordinances". Her husband was granted land "as near Athlone or other places in Connaught, where she shall desire . . . to the end that it may afford the petitioner the better conveniency of repairing neare to such places where the Gospel is preached". This was also signed by Thomas Herbert in Dublin on 6 October 1654.

Another and greater problem for the Council was how to deal with the numerous cases of Cromwellian officers and soldiers who had been granted lands, but who had married Irish girls. Cromwell's soldiers were forbidden under heavy penalties to take Irish girls as wives. For any amours during their service they were severely flogged, and as the soldiers pretended that the Irish girls they married were converts to the Protestant religion, Ireton issued an order declaring: "whereas diverse officers, souldiers of the army doe daily intermarry with the women of this nation who are papists who only for some corrupt or carnell ends and it is to be feared, pretend to bee otherwise, and who while remaining or not being really brought off those false ways in which they doe walk, are declared by the Lord to be the people of His wrath." On Ireton's death the order seems to have been honoured more in the breach than in the observance. After much debate, the Council finally adjudged that the Irish girls were *de facto* Protestants, and allowed them to settle on the lands.

Before the lands of those transplanted could be settled, a survey had to be carried out. Sir William Petty, the physician to the parliamentary army in Ireland, was chosen to do the work. He was a remarkable man for his times. Not only was he a doctor, he was also a surveyor and one of the leading mathematicians of his age, a shipbuilder (he invented the double-hulled vessel) and an ironmaster, who set up extensive ironworks in Kerry after being granted land there. He was appointed chief surveyor at a religious ceremony in Dublin Castle, attended by the high-ranking officers of the army. Colonel Tomlison invoked the blessing of God on so great an undertaking. Dr Petty was himself a freethinker and scoffed at all forms of religion and at the different sects, which he described as "worms and maggots in the guts of the Commonwealth". He began his survey immediately after his appointment, the field work being carried out by soldiers under his supervision. Petty described some of the difficulties in a foreword to this work: "Upon the field work, it being a matter of great drudgery to wade through bogs in winter, climb rocks, fare and lodge hard."

There was also the constant threat of attack from the Tories, as the outlawed Irish soldiers still at large were called. The Reverend Aubrey Gwynn, in his "Cromwell's Policy of Transportation" (1830–31), called the Down Survey "a work of violence" as it was stipulated right from the beginning that Petty was to have the protection of military forces. This was only partially successful, as in March 1655, eight of his men were captured by a band of Tories led by "Blind Donough" O'Derrick. They were taken to a nearby wood and hanged. "Blind Donough" and his followers were later betrayed by one of their number, tracked down by units of the parliamentary army and hanged in front of the house where they were taken. Not satisfied with hanging the culprits, the government ordered that their nearest relatives were to be transported to Barbados, including the wife and daughter of "Blind Donough".

When Dr Petty concluded his survey, Ireland was then the best-mapped country in Europe. Petty estimated that the population of Ireland in 1641 was 1,668,000. Eleven years later, by 1652, it was reduced to 1,100,000: one third of the population, 568,000, had perished in that time, of whom 504,000 were Irish "wasted by the sword, plague, famine and hardship". He goes on to give a graphic description of the country: "The said 1,100,000 do live in about 200,000 families in Houses, whereof there are but about 16,000 which have more than one Chimney in each house, and about 24,000 which have but one, all the other Houses being 160,000 are nasty, wretched cabins, without Chimney, Window or Door, and worse than those of the savage Americans."

With the completion of the Down Survey the settlement of the most fertile lands of Munster, Leinster and Ulster could begin. Cromwell was carrying out King James I's advice: "Plant Ireland with Puritans and root out the Papists and then secure it." The army were the first to be allocated lands. The Adventurers (the city merchants who had subscribed money for the suppression of the rebellion of 1641) were now allocated their portions, but it was found that after all the settlements were met there was still some land available.

As early as 1650 Cromwell had written to some of the leading settlers in New England begging them to return and recolonise Ireland, "that desolate Ireland which hath been drenched and steeped in blood may be moistened and soaked with the waters of the sanctuary". Their letter of reply said: "hoping that as we came by a call of God to serve him here, so if the Lord's mind shall clearly appear to give us a sufficient call to remove into Ireland to serve

Him there, we shall cheerfully and thankfully embrace the same". But it seems that the call of God was not strong enough, because they went on to make certain stipulations, among them being an objection to the presence of native Irish living amongst them. At any rate none of them ever came to Ireland. Cromwell also tried to inveigle Dutch and German Protestants to take up land in Ireland, with similar results.

Because no English labour was available, the English settlers needed Irish labourers to work the land as the "hewers of wood and drawers of water", so they were forced to employ Irish Catholics. This was also the case in the towns where apothecaries, butchers, bakers, carpenters, chandlers, coopers, harnessmakers, masons, shoemakers, tailors and suchlike were needed. In a few instances medical men were given certificates exempting them from transplantation. One such instance was that of Dr Minshinogue who was saved from transplantation by a Colonel Jepson of Mallow Castle, County Cork, who appealed successfully on his behalf. He was permitted to continue his practice but not to dwell in any garrison in Cork.

By the end of April 1654 all those forced to transplant had done so. Despite Cromwell's assurance in 1649 that "the Nobility, Gentry, and Commons of Ireland as have not been actors in this Rebellion, they shall and may expect the protection of their Goods, Liberties, and Lives". Three quarters of the population had been uprooted and forced into the remaining fourth of the country. A worse fate awaited those who refused to transplant: hanging or transportation to the "Tobacco Island"—Barbados.

CHAPTER FOUR

The Ethnic Cleansing of Ireland

"We have three beasts to destroy which lay burdensome upon us. The first is the wolf on whom we lay five pounds a head if a dog, and ten pounds if a bitch; the second beast is a priest, on whose head we lay ten pounds, and if he be eminent more. The third beast is the Tory, and on his head, if he be a public Tory, we lay ten pounds, and if he is a private Tory, we pay 40 shillings."

Speech of Major Morgan, MP for Wicklow, 10 June 1657

THE LANDLORDS WHO refused to transplant and whose properties had been seized by Cromwellian settlers were known as the Tories by the English. They took to the impassable bogs, woods and mountains with their families and retainers. They were often joined by soldiers who had refused to go abroad or had returned secretly from France and Spain to continue the struggle. From their retreats they waged a savage guerrilla campaign against the usurpers, driving off their livestock, setting fire to their property and, if the opportunity arose, killing the settlers.

Colonel Lawrence, the chief commissioner sitting in Loughrea, wrote of the Tories:

> The Irish had been driven from garrisons, castles, and places of strength to bogs and woods. There they

lurked, watching for opportunities to commit murders and outrages . . . Sundry persons were daily taken out of their houses in the night time, and sometimes set upon as they travel upon the highway, or are surprised by these desperate persons, and carried into woods and bogs, and there murdered or kept in a miserable manner, in cold, nakedness, and hunger, and their houses burned, and their goods carried away until they pay a ransom.

Several such cases are recorded in the State Papers for Ireland 1652–59. No planters were safe except those that lived in fortified castles, and even they were liable to be murdered. Lawrence gives an account of two such actions by the Tories:

There was an incident of one gentleman living in a strong castle and sitting with his wife and children around the fire one evening, when some person whose voice he knew, called him by name to come to his gate to speak with him. The poor gentleman, expecting no danger in an area where there were no enemy, presently went to the door where he was murdered . . . Another gentleman, walking in his gardens in the daytime was also found murdered.

Colonel Lawrence went on to give reasons why the Irish refused to transplant, preferring the misery and danger of their outlawed existence to Connaught:

[T]he true reason of the dislike of the Irish to transplant was that they looked to their national interest, and discerned that the transplantation laid the axe at the root of the tree of their future hopes of their recovering their lost ground; and besides their unwillingness to quit the possession of their ancient inheritances, and to be settled upon other men's inheritances in Connaught, they foresaw, perhaps, that the Connaught proprietor might bid them such welcome as they would bid the soldier and adventurer upon their lands.

The government adopted more stringent methods to hunt down and exterminate the Tories. Bounties were offered to Irishmen who became collaborators. They were recruited to track down and kill or capture Tories. Forty shillings was to be paid to any countryman who brought to the nearest garrison commander the head of a Tory, and the life of any Tory was to be spared if he brought in the heads of two fellow Tories. Arms and ammunition were occasionally entrusted to these Irish quislings to track down Tories, just as they were employed to hunt and kill wolves. It is possible that sometimes they may have killed people other than Tories; they could kill any Irishman and claim that he was a Tory.

There are records of men claiming dispensation from transplantation to Connaught by engaging to keep their districts clear of Tories. Probably the most prominent of these men was Lord Ikerrin, on whose behalf even Cromwell himself intervened to prevent his transplantation. Lord Ikerrin had gone to London in 1656 and through influence was able to have an audience with Cromwell. The Lord Protector then wrote to the Lord Deputy and Council of Ireland as follows:

My Lord and Gentlemen,

We being informed by several persons, and also by certificates from several officers under our command in Ireland, that the Lord Viscount Ikerrin hath been of later times serviceable to suppress the Tories; and we being very sensible of the extreme poor and miserable condition in which his lordship now is, even to the want of sustenance to support his life; we could not but commiserate his sad and distressed condition by helping him to a little relief, without which he could neither subsist here nor return back to Ireland; and therefore do earnestly desire you to take him into speedy consideration, by allowing him some reasonable proportion of his estate without transplanting him, or otherwise to make some provision for him and his family elsewhere, and to allow him some competent pension or money out of the revenue. Indeed he is a miserable object of pity, and therefore we desire that care be taken of him, and that he be not suffered to perish for want of a subsistence: And rest, your loving friend, Oliver P.

Despite the Lord Protector's plea Lord Ikerrin did not get back his estate. It had been seized by a Cromwellian officer, Colonel Hierome Sankey, who was criticised by Sir William Petty "for his unhandsome dealings with his soldiers in the matter of Lismalin Park"—this being the estate of Lord Ikerrin. There is no record of Lord Ikerrin's ever getting back his land.

A man named Charles Kavanagh, who owned 1400 acres in the county of Carlow, did retain his lands in return for destroying Tories in that county and in the adjoining counties of Wicklow, Wexford and Kilkenny. Men in other counties also managed to retain their lands by hunting down and killing or capturing Tories. Hunts were organised with dogs, half mastiff and half bloodhound specially imported from England, to track down the Tories. Meets were arranged at designated places, as foxhound meets are held today. They were accompanied by recreant Irish servants who preceded them. Once a quarry was sighted, the hounds were loosed and bounded forward, bringing down their prey. More often than not, this would be just a peasant trying to eke out a subsistence. The real Tories prepared mantraps for their hunters by leading them into bogs or quagmires and then slaughtering them at their leisure.

In 1655 Vincent Gookin, a Protestant landowner from Macroom, published a pamphlet called "The Great Case of Transplantation discussed by a well-wisher to the good of the Commonwealth of England", in which he wrote that because Irish husbandry was being wrecked by wars and transplantations, the Irish became brigands as their only alternative was starvation. Such an argument may seem obvious to the modern reader, but it was at that time considered a radical notion.

Hanging was the penalty for not transplanting, and gallows were erected in every garrison town, to which those who did not transplant were brought and, after a mock trial, hanged. The records in the State Papers for 1655 give many instances. Two of the first were Daniel Fitzpatrick and another unnamed man, who on 25 March were condemned to death by the commissioners in Kilkenny and duly hanged. Dr Petty records the trial of a Mr Hetherington before a court martial sitting in St Patrick's Cathedral, Dublin. He was an extensive landowner and had refused to transplant. The officers found him guilty, and he was hanged in public on 3 April. Placards were attached to his chest and back reading that he was executed "for not transplanting". If Hetherington's hanging was meant as an example for others, it did not work. The gaols were full of people who refused to transplant and were awaiting trials.

Because of the fears inspired by the attacks of the Tories, settlers were leaving their estates and moving either to garrison towns or returning to England. The commissioners decided on a new policy of depopulating whole areas in which these attacks occurred. If the culprits who committed a crime were not apprehended, then four or five of the most prominent men in the area were taken and hanged on the spot and the remainder transported to Barbados. In just one instance in which this policy was put into practice, two Irishmen, Denis Brennan and Murtagh Turner, who had been troopers in the Cromwellian army under Colonel Hewson, were engaged in repairing houses of people who had been transplanted in readiness for their new occupiers. They were murdered by a band of local Tories. Four Catholics were hanged and thirty-seven people—three priests, twenty-one women and thirteen men—were, on 27

November 1655, delivered to a Captain Coleman of a Wexford frigate for transportation to Barbados. The names of the priests were given as James Tuite, Robert Keegan and John Foley.

The transported also included all the inhabitants of Lackagh Castle, Kildare, which was owned by the Fitzgerald family. Henry Fitzgerald and his wife were both over eighty years of age, but this did not save them. It is difficult to imagine of what use they could possibly have been to a planter in Barbados, assuming that they survived the voyage. Their son Maurice, their daughters Margary and Brigid, together with Mary, the widow of their eldest son Henry, and with their manservant and maidservant were among the list of the thirty-seven taken to be transported. The irony of this particular event was that the Fitzgerald family had been exempt from transplantation and themselves had suffered depredation at the hands of the Tories. This fact did not save them either, and they were consigned to a local gaol to await shipment with a cargo of other transportees, in a vessel belonging to a Mr Norton, a Bristol merchant and sugar planter.

However, the officers and soldiers due to occupy the lands owned by the Irish who refused to transplant were in no mood for further delays, as the following letter shows. It was apparently written by a senior officer and published in *Mercurius Politicus* in London. Dated 4 March 1654, and written in Athy, it reads as follows:

> I have only to acquaint you, that the time prescribed for the transplantation of the Irish proprietors, and those that have been in arms and abettors of the rebellion, being near at hand, the officers are resolved to fill the gaols and to seize them; by which this bloody people will know that they [the officers] are not degenerated from English principles; though I presume we shall be very tender of hanging any except leading men . . . yet we shall make no scruple of sending them to the West Indies.

Henry Cromwell, then deputy for Ireland, in a letter dated 12 March 1656, addressed to his father, stated that he had already secured some thousand Irishmen who had been in arms "upon the account of non-transplanting". He went on: "It was offered to His Highness [Oliver Cromwell], they being clearly at your mercy as they are, that it would be very good service to the public, and tend much to the future quiet and peace of this nation, to send these men either to some of your foreign plantations or to some other service."

His father, sensing the significance of this, replied on 26 August:

> Whereas we have daily intelligence that the old malig-
> nant party [the royalists] by confederacy with Spain,
> are forming a design to invade this Commonwealth
> with foreign forces, and at the same time to raise up
> a rebellion within our bowels . . . we have thought it
> necessary that some chief persons of the Irish be
> secured, and to that purpose you are to give immedi-
> ate orders for the apprehending and securing in some
> safe place, as to you shall seem fit, such of the heads
> and other considerable persons in Ireland as you shall
> judge to be dangerous.

It is evident that Oliver Cromwell was referring to the Irish who had been allowed to go to Spain and were now returning to take up the old fight with backing from their host country.

Immediately after the end of the war in Ireland, priests, "the second of the beasts that lay heavily upon us", to quote Major Morgan, had a price of £10 put on their heads and were hunted down like wolves. However the Commissioners for Ireland realised that here was a source of manpower which could be profitably used in Barbados, and so issued an order requiring "priests or other persons in Papish orders" to prepare for transportation. It continued: "And it is further ordered that such said persons and all other priests and others in Popish orders, as shall not come in and render themselves as above said, shall be apprehended and proceeded against according to former Declarations published in their behalf." It was a question of "heads I win, tails you lose". The Catholic clergy of Ireland knew that in addition to the horrors of transportation, they would be treated with particular savagery at their destination. Many of them therefore chose to disguise themselves as beggars or out of work labourers and were arrested and transported as "rogues and vagabonds". In this way they were at least able to minister to their flock undetected.

Many priests sought refuge among the Tories, sharing their hardships and ministering to their religious needs. If a Tory band was captured, the men and women were marked for transport to Barbados, but the priests were invariably executed. One such instance of a priest hiding out was that of Father Forde, who concealed himself among the rushes and tall grass of an immense bog, where he celebrated mass for the local people. Another priest, Father Neterville, hid himself in his family's tomb and emerged at night to celebrate mass.

There was one proviso about the priests who were to be transported to the colonies: they had to be young and fit. The president of Connaught, General Coote, was instructed

> . . . to take care that the priests or friars that are now imprisoned in Galway that are above the age of forty years, be forthwith banished into France, Portugal or other neighbouring kingdoms in amity with this Commonwealth, and that the rest of the priests, that are under the age of forty years, be herewith shipped away to Barbados, or other American plantations, and likewise to give public notice that in case of any of the said priests and friars shall at any time return into this nation, without special licence, they shall be proceeded against according to the laws now in force.

General orders for the transportation of priests were issued in 1654–55. Officers and soldiers of the parliamentary army were employed to track down and capture the priests. Entries in the State Order Books show that those engaged in the task were paid a bounty, "over and above" their ordinary pay. Here is just one example: "Peter Power be paid five pounds for the arrest of a priest, the priest to be sent to Galway to Colonel Stubbers, who is to take care that this priest, with other priests in custody in that town, be sent to Barbados by 1 July 1654."

A letter dated 8 November 1654 and written by Thomas Herbert, the clerk of the Council, Dublin Castle, to Daniel Searle, the governor of Barbados, confirms the Council of Ireland's decision to transport priests:

> His Highness and Council for the Affairs of Ireland have ordered Captain John Norris to take aboard his ship divers Irish men and women (such as by the Justices are found to be vagabond and idlers) to be exported to the Barbados or some other of the English Plantation Islands of the Cariba or thereabouts; and also three Popish priests who are likewise to be there landed. It is the desire of the Council that care may be taken in especial concerning those three priests that they may be so employed as they may not be at liberty to return again into this nation, where that sort of a people are able to do much mischief, by having so great an influence over the popish Irish here, and of alienating their affection from the present Government.

The names of two of these priests were given as Thomas FitzNicholas and Brother John Stafford; the identity of the third is not known. The letter was delivered to the governor when the ship docked in Barbados sometime during the end of December.

Daniel Searle, a virulently anti-papist Puritan, was less

than pleased to receive such a letter. He considered priests "fomentors of rebellion" and echoed the clerk's sentiments that "that sort of people are able to do much mischief". Searle had to take into account that there was a large Irish slave population on the island, the majority of whom held an endemic hatred of the English.

Although Daniel Searle objected only to priests as transportees, the Puritan settlers of New England objected to *any* Irish people being sent to them, as the following act passed in the General Court of Massachusetts on 29 October 1654 shows: "This Court, considering the cruel and malignant spirit that has from time to time been manifest in the Irish nation against this English nation, do hereby declare their prohibition of bringing any Irish, men, women or children into this jurisdiction, on the penalty of 50 pounds sterling to each inhabitant who shall buy of a merchant, shipmaster or other agent, any such person or persons so transported by them." The signatories of this act in an addendum asked the English Parliament "to prevent the importation of the Irish priests and convicts that are yearly power'd upon us, and to make provision against the growth of this pernicious evil".

Because of the objections lodged by the governors of the plantations to the admission of any priests, a new plan had to be devised by Parliament. Cabins were built for them on the Aran Islands and on the island of Inisboffin, off the coast of Connemara. At least there a watchful eye could be kept on them. Soldiers continuously patrolled the islands. No boats were allowed to land, except those that brought provisions for the priests and garrison, and they had absolutely no contact with the outside world. These islands were, to all intents and purposes, concentration camps.

CHAPTER FIVE

The Irish in Barbados

*"I have seen an overseer beat a white servant with a cane
about the head, till the blood has flowed, for a fault that is not
worth the speaking of."*
Richard Ligon, A True and Exact History of the Island of
Barbados (1657)

THE ISLAND, WHICH the bishops at Clonmacnoise and
Cromwell referred to as the "Tobacco Island", had
been settled by the English since 1627. Long before
Cromwell ever set foot in Ireland, many of the bishops'
flock had been lured there as indentured servants with false
promises of free housing, good wages and a plot of land at
the end of their indentures.

Barbados was discovered almost by accident. In 1536 a
Portugese ship commanded by Pedro a Campos visited the
island en route to Brazil. Although he was not interested in
settling the island, it is thought that he may have left pigs
on the island to act as a possible later food supply. Then,
in 1605, the captain of a British ship, the *Olive Blossom*,
claimed the island for James I.

Sir William Courteen, a partner in the Anglo-Dutch
trading firm of Courteen Brothers, with extensive holdings
in Brazil, was one of the great merchant adventurers of the

early seventeenth century. The firm's vessels made a regular passage between South America and England. Early in 1625, one of its ships, commanded by Master Captain John Powell, was blown off course on a return voyage from Perambuco (now Recife) in Brazil to England and sought shelter in one of the bays of an island which was not marked on his map. He and some of his men rowed ashore, found the island uninhabited with good soil, well watered, with sheltered harbours and also plenty of timber for building. He immediately took possession of it in the name of his master, and erected a crude sign: "James, K of E and of this Island."

Unfortunately for him and for Courteen, on his return journey his ship touched in at St Christopher (now St Kitts), one of the Leeward Islands. His men, incautiously, talked about their discovery in one of the taverns, and thus set off a chain of events which had repercussions in Barbados and in England for many years to come.

When Powell reached London he informed his master of his find. Courteen immediately asked James I for a patent to settle the island. Unfortunately the king died before it was granted. Nevertheless, he set up a syndicate of merchants which contributed £10,000 for this purpose. In 1627, John Powell's brother, Henry, set out for Barbados with eighty settlers and ten slaves. By 1628, 1600 "young gentlemen", as Courteen described them, had arrived there, built houses and fortifications and planted tobacco. They named the first town Jamestown (now Bridgetown) and began to send large cargoes of tobacco to England.

In the strict judicial sense, this settlement of Courteen's was illegal, and unfortunately for him, another merchant adventurer was active in the Leewards. Sir William Warner had first attempted a settlement in Guinea in 1620, but found the climate there so bad and the Spanish such a constant threat that he only spent two seasons there. Sailing back to England he searched for a suitable island in the Leeward chain and found St Christopher, a beautiful island, well suited for growing tobacco. He took it over, and on his arrival in London also formed a syndicate and returned to the island with some 500 planters. They began by expelling all the native Caribs. A party of French privateers arrived soon after, and the settlers agreed to give them half the island in return for their help against any future Carib attacks.

To make his occupation of St Christopher legal, Warner sought a patent from the new king, Charles I, through the influence of the king's favourite courtier, James Hay, Earl of Carlisle, and it was on his recommendation that a commission was granted to Warner, naming him governor of the four islands of St Christopher, Nevis, Montserrat and Barbados.

Sir William Courteen paid dearly for his neglect in obtaining a patent from King James' son. Perhaps he thought that his lack of a patent would be overlooked in court circles. However, he did not take into consideration the cupidity of courtiers who surrounded the king, or indeed the greed of the London tobacco merchants. Courteen now applied to King Charles I for a patent to make his occupation of the island legal, but this was refused. Then began a court battle which William Courteen lost. His health shattered, he returned to England and died in debt.

In May 1629 the Earl of Carlisle, the winner of the court case against Courteen and now owner of the island, appointed Sir William Tufton, younger brother of the Earl of Thanet, as governor. Barbados in its early years was a harsh place in which to make a living. The bush, scrub and forests had to be cleared before any tobacco could be planted. This was certainly not the place for young gentlemen brought up in the court of Charles I; yeomen with strong backs and willing hands were needed.

Tufton, the first of a long, unbroken line of governors, brought with him over 1000 settlers from England, many of them "young gentlemen" who began importing indentured servants at their own expense to work on their plantations. Tufton did his best to alleviate the harsh conditions of the indentured servants then on the island, but his efforts were thwarted by the London merchants who had been granted 10,000 acres of the best land by the Earl of Carlisle in repayment of his gambling debts. These merchants regarded Barbados simply as a place from which to reap large profits by growing tobacco and began even to recruit convicts and other undesirables from England to work their plantations for them.

Because the London merchants thought Tufton too soft on the indentured servants, they persuaded Carlisle to send out a man named Henry Hawley as governor. Hawley was a despot and ruled Barbados for the next ten years as if it were his own fief. When Tufton and many of the other planters objected to his tyrannical use of power, Hawley simply arrested Tufton and his followers, rigged a court martial composed of his own supporters who found Tufton guilty of treason, and had him shot the following day. Many of Tufton's supporters were hanged. Hawley handed out plantations to his own supporters, while evicting those who held land from Courteen. These lands he appropriated for himself.

Hawley levied taxes on every resident of Barbados, and those who could not pay the forty pounds weight of tobacco were imprisoned. He maintained a harsh discipline on the island, and hanging, flogging, branding and excessive fines became a regular occurrence. An Anglican priest, the Reverend Thomas Lane, who visited Barbados in 1637, described the island as, "a place where ignorance of the laws of God and man doeth domineer".

A planter named Thomas Verney wrote to his father asking him to send out fifty cases of good spirit. "I make no question," he writes, "but you will have great gaynes from them . . . they are generally such drunkards in this island that they will find coppers to buy their drinks although they go without themselves. Such is their lewdness and their ill qualities in this and all other islands." Hawley himself was, among other things, a drunkard and no doubt obtained some of Verney's good spirit, as he gave him 100 acres of prime land.

Alcoholism seemed to be prevalent on the island, as Verney wrote to his father in another letter: "I have seen upon the Sabbath day, as I have been walking to church, first one, presently another lie in the highways so drunk that here be . . . land crabs that have bit off, some their fingers, some their toes and hath killed some before they have wakened."

A visitor to the island, Sir Henry Colt, wrote as early as 1631: "You are devourers upp of strong waters." He also condemned the slovenly management of some plantations: "[Y]our ground and plantations shows what you are, they lie like ye ruines of some village lately buried."

Finally, the planters of Barbados revolted against Hawley's autocratic regime and sent a petition to the Earl of Carlisle for his dismissal. Twice he was recalled to England to answer charges of swindling and using the supplies sent out by Carlisle for his own use. He managed to talk himself out of trouble on both occasions and each time was returned as governor. He set up a parliament made up of the most prominent planters on the island, most of them cronies of his (the speaker was his brother-in-law). He was finally taken prisoner for the third time, by the king's commissioners in 1640, to answer further charges of mismanagement. He must have led a charmed life for, instead of being committed to the Tower, he remained at liberty and almost twenty years later, in 1667, returned yet again to Barbados, where he became a member of the Assembly and even regained possession of his sequestered lands. He died in Barbados in 1677 at the age of eighty, allegedly as a result of falling down the stairs of a brothel in Roebuck Street in Bridgetown when drunk.

Henry Huncks succeeded Hawley as governor, but his reign did not last long; he was recalled to England in 1641 to answer charges of misappropriation. He was succeeded by Philip Bell, and under his just and even-handed rule of nine years the island prospered. He gave the elected parliament, now known as the House of Assembly, the power to pass its own laws. He reorganised the militia, whose senior officers were all Hawley's appointees. He also enforced regular attendance at divine services, and recognised the Church of England as the established church. During his governorship there was a large influx of both planters and indentured labourers.

The planters of Barbados, the "young gentlemen" as Courteen called them, many of them alcoholics and certainly none of them accustomed to manual labour, had no intention of working the land themselves. They recruited what were known as indentured servants in England, Wales, Scotland and Ireland.

An indenture was a legal contract binding an employee to his master for a limited period. The document stated the duties of the master and the duties of the employee, and was inscribed in duplicate on both ends of the paper. The paper was then torn in two along a jagged line, so that each of the contracting parties could have a copy. This indented or serrated edge between the two copies gave it the name "indenture". Even the most illiterate could see that when the serrated edges of the contract were fitted together, they matched. At the end of their indentures they were promised what was called their "indenture dues": a small piece of land and some tools for cultivation. Indentures could be signed for any number of years from five to ten, but seven years was the usual length.

There were three main types of indentured labour:
1. "Freewillers", who deliberately sold themselves under indenture.
2. "Redemptioners", who were persuaded or duped into signing indentures and who were sold for cash on arrival.
3. "Spiriters", who were kidnapped by merchants' agents

70

or ships' captains. These operated mainly in London and in the seaport towns of Bristol and Liverpool.

Many of those kidnapped were children, some as young as eight. One of these spiriters boasted that he had sold an average of 500 children a year over a period of twelve years. Another claimed that he had captured and sold 850 in a single year. There was one case of a girl named Alice Deakins who was kidnapped at the age of sixteen from London. She managed to escape and was able to identify and lay a charge against her kidnapper. He was arrested, tried and convicted, but his sentence was a paltry twelve pence.

The agents and captains in England and Ireland used every trick to inveigle working-class people to transport to Barbados. They painted a rosy picture of a good life under the sun, good food and accommodation, and most important of all, the prospect of a plot of land when their indentures terminated. Whole families from the north of England and from the poorer areas of Ireland, Wales and Scotland signed indentures. They were mainly manual workers and tradesmen: butchers, bakers, carpenters, shoemakers and labourers were shipped to the promised land. Those on parish relief were often denied it and were forced to sign indentures or starve.

The first Irish indentured servants of which we have any direct knowledge were shipped from Kinsale in 1636. Among the High Court of Admiralty papers in the Public Records Office in London there is a letter written to an American ship owner in Virginia, Anthony Craddock, by one of his captains, Joseph West. His orders were to sail to Kinsale in Ireland and there pick up a cargo of 120 Irish indentured servants and bring them to America.

Captain Joseph West set sail in his ship, the *Abraham*, and arrived in Kinsale on 28 April 1636. On enquiring he found that a ship owned by Dutch-Jewish merchants had just beaten him to it and had signed on most of the available labour force for transportation to Barbados. He wrote to the ship's owner that "a flymishe shippe of 140 tonnes or thereabouts from Amsterdam hath gonne from here with one hundred and twenty to one hundred and forty persons, men and women". Captain West found the utmost difficulty in obtaining indentured labour. As soon as his ship anchored he caused "the drume to be beatten and gave warninge to all those that disposed to goe as servants to Virginia should repare to Kinsale where I lay and upon conditions according to the country I would entertain all such". Response was slow, and Captain West, finding that he could not get enough voluntary indentured servants in Kinsale, employed agents to go inland to induce by any means or to kidnap people to fill his allotment. We even have the name of one such agent, a Thomas Buckley of Bandon, who was paid "a pinte of wine and some shugar" for every person thus procured. By October Captain West had a cargo of sixty-one, forty-one men and twenty women, all between the ages of seventeen and thirty-five. He wrote to the ship's owner: "We dowe entertayne both men and women, and have entertayned also some persons, very lustye and strong bodies, which I hope be meyns to set off to the best advantage." It is very probable that the "lustye and strong bodies" were kidnapped around Kinsale as West then found himself imprisoned by the mayor for several days until these were released.

He now had to procure food for the journey and obtain clothing for the remaining indentured servants, most of whom were in rags. He had garments made of coarse linen by a tailor named Neal Hughes, who charged him the sum of 7s. 6d. for each garment, an exorbitant sum for those days.

Captain West set sail for Virginia on 22 November, the worst possible time of the year for an Atlantic crossing. Due to the bad weather he put in at Cowes, where he obtained a "mydwiffe" to visit the women servants. She found three pregnant and a fourth with "the French dizeas". The three pregnant women were put ashore with a shilling each; the other woman was left stranded without a penny.

West set sail again but found that owing to the battering it was receiving his ship had become "a weake and leakie vessel" and he could not reach Virginia. He decided to run for Barbados, where he dropped anchor on 25 January 1637. Eight of the servants had died on the journey, but it took him only two days to sell the remaining fifty-three. He wrote to Anthony Craddock, the owner, that he had sold "ten to the Governor of Barbados for 450 pounds of sugar apiece, and all the rest for 500 pounds apiece". When his ship was repaired he was instructed to return to London to sell his sugar and then to proceed to Kinsale in an endeavour to procure another cargo of indentured servants.

Richard Povey, a rich planter of the period, wrote about this trade: "The ship owners who transport these persons make a gainful business out of it . . . Many of them considered the charge of the passage and disbursement as a debt which entitled them to claim a sort of property in the bodies of their passengers, and to dispose of them among the planters. Merchants thought of their human cargoes strictly in market terms, with payment either in bills of exchange or in colonial products, cotton or tobacco."

The ships that carried them were between 140 and 200 tons, and the passage from England to Barbados took between eight and ten weeks. They frequently put in at Madeira, Cape Verde or the Azores before setting out for Barbados. Merchants and ships' captains expected some deaths, and a loss of 20 per cent was considered normal. Thomas Rous, a planter who sailed to Barbados in 1638, complained of the high mortality rate. His ship held 350 passengers, of whom two or three were thrown overboard almost every day. Eighty of the indentured servants, men and women, died on that voyage.

An English economist, Josiah Child, writing in the seventeenth century, had no high opinion of indentured labour:

Virginia and Barbados were first peopled by a sort of loose vagrant people, vicious and destitute of means to live at home, (being either unfit for labour, or such as could find none to employ them.) Merchants and masters of ships by their agents (of spirits as they were called) gathered up about the streets of London and other places, clothed and transported to be employed on plantations; and these, I say, had there been no English foreign plantations, could never at home do service to their country, but must have come to be hanged or starved or died untimely of some miserable diseases, that proceed from want and vice.

Richard Ligon, the first historian of Barbados, writing in 1657, gave an account of the indentured servants' introduction to their daily life on a plantation in Barbados:

Upon the arrival of any ship... the Planters go aboard; and having bought such of them as they like, send them with a guide to his Plantation; and being come, commands them instantly to make their Cabins, which they not knowing how to do, are to be advised by other of their servants, that are their Seniors; but, if they be churlish, and will not show them or if materials be wanting to make them Cabins, then they are to lye on the ground that night. These Cabins are to be made of sticks, withs, and Plantine leaves, under some little shade that may keep the rain off; their Suppers being a few Potatoes ... and water and Mobbie for drink. The next day they are rung out with a Bell to work, at six a clock in the morning ... till the Bell ring again, which is at eleven a clock; and then they return and are set to dinner, either with a mess of Loblolly, Bonavist, or Potatoes.

Loblolly was a dreary maize-based seaman's gruel. Slaves disliked it so much that at first sight of it they cried out in unison: "Oh, no loblolly, no loblolly." Bonavist was boiled sweet potatoes.

Almost from the earliest days of the settlement of Barbados, the indentured servants were treated as little more than slaves. For any sign of insubordination or malingering they were flogged with cowhide whips, leaving deep scars. Most of the indentured servants were terrified of making any complaints to the magistrates, because the men who sat on the bench were also planters, who responded by calling such complaints "malicious", and very often increased an indentured servant's time by one year or more.

It was natural that the conditions of a servant under indenture on a plantation varied according to the kind of master who held his indenture. Most of the planters at the time were brutal and inconsiderate. The lash was in daily use as the servants were forced to ever greater efforts to get the most work possible out of them. In 1648 indentured servants conspired to kill their masters and take over the island. This conspiracy was apparently led by Irish indentured servants. Ligon described it:

> Their sufferings being grown to a great height, and their daily complainings to one another ... being spread throughout the Island; at the last, some amongst them whose spirits were not able to endure such slavery, resolved to break through it, or dye in the act; and so conspired with some others ... so that a day was appointed to fall upon their Masters, and cut all their throats, and by that means, to make themselves not only freemen, but Masters of the Island. And so closely was this plot carried, as no discovery was made, till the day before they were to put it in act; and then one of them, either by the failing of his courage, or some new obligation from the love of his Master, revealed the long plotted conspiracy; and so by this timely advertisement, the Masters were saved.

All the conspirators were arrested, and a special act was passed on 4 October 1649 setting up a Council of War "for the trial of persons guilty of the late insurrection". Eighteen were hanged, drawn and quartered, and their heads were set on pikes in prominent positions in Bridgetown.

CHAPTER SIX

The Irish White Slave Trade

"[Y]oung maidens of noble families were despoiled of their possessions and dragged almost naked and piercing heaven with their shrieks to a ship bound for the West Indies. . . "
Cardinal Giovanni Battista Rinuccini, papal nuncio to the Confederation of Kilkenny (1645–48)

THE ETHNIC CLEANSING of Ireland may be said to have begun on 24 August 1652. On that date, there was put into operation the most thorough and ruthless transfer of the Irish people to overseas colonies ever undertaken by any English leader. A proclamation was issued which gave ultimate power to the Commissioners of Ireland to seize and transport anybody of whatever rank who was judged dangerous to the Commonwealth. Into this category fell landlords who refused to transplant, some of whom were not even Tories, soldiers who had not emigrated to join foreign armies and the dependants of the soldiers who had gone abroad. As we have seen, the majority of the Irish "swordsmen", as the English called them, who had gone abroad to join the armies of several foreign countries not at war with England were not allowed to take their dependants with them. Therefore a vast number of women were left behind in a destitute situation. An order was passed by the Council: "That Irishwomen, as being too numerous now—and therefore, exposed to prostitution—be sold to merchants, and transported to Virginia, New England, or other countries, where they may support themselves by their labour." This was most probably the most cynical piece of legislation passed by the Council of Ireland. While it was true that a few Irish women married or prostituted themselves with Cromwellian soldiers, the penalties for doing so were very severe for both parties.

It was no difficult matter, at this time, to round up plenty of women and children, as there were crowds of young widows and deserted wives and sons and daughters wandering about in the neighbourhood of cities and towns, without any visible means of support. It is not surprising that they gravitated towards the towns and cities. The countryside was a wilderness. Very little was left growing after the Cromwellian soldiers had devastated it with fire and with the scythes that Cromwell had thoughtfully provided for just this purpose. Famine was endemic, and some writers have mentioned that cannibalism was rife. One such writer, George Bennett, in his history of Bandon, stated, allegedly quoting from old documents, "The few persons that were occasionally to be met with in the rural parts were wandering orphans, whose fathers had embarked for Poland or Spain, and whose mothers had died of hunger; or were miserable old people, who would quarrel over a putrid carcass raked from a stagnant pool; and some of whom were seen to eat human flesh, cut from the corpse of a fellow-creature, that lay broiling on the fire before them."

The work of rounding up people for transportation was carried out very thoroughly by government agents throughout the country. These "man-catchers", as they were called, were mounted and armed, with long whips to herd the unfortunate people into the holding-pens outside the cities and towns—much as cattle were driven to the fairs in Ireland in the recent past.

Here they were branded with the initials of the ship that would take them to Barbados or Virginia. They were attached together with ropes around their necks and the long march to the seaports in the south of Ireland began. Their meagre food was barely enough to sustain life, and those who fell by the wayside, weak from hunger or disease, were left where they fell.

When they arrived at the seaports of Waterford, Cork, Dungarvan, Passage, Youghal, Kinsale and Bantry, they were flung into filthy goals to await the arrival of the slaveships from Bristol or London. Often a ship would be delayed and the prisoners were then transferred to hulks to await boarding.

There was a special demand for young women, "marriageable and not past breeding", who were eagerly sought after by the sugar planters who, to quote Henry Cromwell, "had only Negresses and Maroon women to solace them". (The Maroons, called by the Spanish *Cimarrones* or "wild men", were descendants of slaves who had fled into the mountains.) The man-catchers were paid £4 or £4 10s. by the ships' captains for every young woman or child. There is a reference to the number of children involved in a note in the Public Records Office held in Kew Gardens. Sir John Clotworthy was given a license by the Board of Trade to transfer 1000 children to Virginia.

The historian Dr Thomas Addis Emmet, in his book *Ireland under English Rule, or a Plea for the Plaintiff*, published in New York in 1903, stated: "Over one hundred thousand young children, who were orphans or had been taken from their Catholic parents, were sent abroad into slavery in the West Indies, Virginia and New England, that they might thus lose their faith and all knowledge of their nationality, for in most instances even their names were changed." This seems to be an exaggerated estimate, but the trade in children and young women flourished.

We have the names of some of these slave ships, primarily from Bristol but some from London, which called at Irish ports: the *Jane*, the *Susan and Mary*, the *Elizabeth* and the *Two Brothers*. These were the same ships that were used to transport black slaves from the West Coast of Africa to the West Indies. The merchants simply switched to the Irish slave trade at a considerable profit to themselves, following a long line of slave merchants who made fortunes from buying slaves in the African market and selling them in Barbados and the colonies of America. So lucrative was this traffic that it was known as "Black Gold". The Portuguese and Spanish found in African slaves a most profitable business, quickly followed by the Dutch. The English were comparative latecomers to the trade. Having delivered their human cargoes to Barbados or Virginia, they returned laden with sugar or tobacco, ready for the return trip.

Cromwell had already received a petition from the Bristol slave merchants to be allowed to participate in this trade. He wrote to Fleetwood, then lord deputy of Ireland: "Some merchants in the city of Bristol have petitioned me for a licence to transport 400 Irish Tories and such other idle and vagrant persons as may be thought fittest to be spared out of Ireland for planting in the Caribbee Islands, which address of theirs I do recommend to your consideration, that their desire therein may be granted in such a way as to you seem fit and expedient."

The Commissioners of Ireland were only too willing to oblige Cromwell by getting rid of a surplus and potentially dangerous population. In January 1654 they ordered the governors of Carlow, Kilkenny, Clonmel, Ross, Wexford and Waterford, "to arrest and deliver to Captains Thomas Morgan, Dudley North and John Johnson, English merchants, all wanderers, men and women and other Irish within their precincts as should not prove that they had such a settled course of industry as yielded them a means of their own to maintain them, all such children as were in hospitals or workhouses, all prisoners, men and women, to be transported to the West Indies". The governors were to transfer the people who were rounded up to the ports of shipping, but these were to be provided for and maintained by the contractors.

Sir William Petty, who had carried out the Down Survey of Ireland, described the Irish slave trade in his book *The Political Anatomy of Ireland* (1672) thus: "The widows and orphans, the deserted wives and families of the swordsmen were kidnapped and transported by the slave trading merchants of Bristol which their previous experience enabled them to organise with advantage to themselves."

In September, a Captain John Vernon was employed by the Commissioners for Ireland and signed a contract on their behalf to supply Mr Sellick and Mr Yoemans, Bristol merchants, with 250 women above the age of twelve years to be found in the country within a twenty miles radius of Cork, Youghal, Kinsale, Waterford and Wexford, and then transport them to Barbados and New England. Lord Broghill, governor of Cork, assured the commissioners that he could find, in a short time, the 250 within the environs of Cork alone.

Elliott O'Donnell, in his book *The Irish Abroad* (1915), gives an account of the fate of young girls seized for transhipment abroad. While in the majority of cases those destined for the plantations were put aboard ships in Irish ports, O'Donnell gives an example of Irish girls shipped from Cork to Bristol and there put aboard a slave ship. It is a harrowing account:

> Between the years 1651 to 1654 over 40,000 Celtic Irishmen marched away, to die with all their accustomed gallantry—many winning unperishable renown—in the services of France, Spain, Poland and Italy. Having thus succeeded in deporting the men, Cromwell next turned his attention to the women. Hearing that the planters in New England and the West Indies were weary of maroons, and would pay any price for a white woman, Puritan

Cromwell at once volunteered to supply their needs. Gangs of his soldiers invaded Connaught, and pouncing on all the women and girls they could find, drove them in gangs to Cork. It was the work of 1603 over again, only on a much larger and even more revolting scale. The young and pretty women were frequently violated, the older and uglier beaten and branded. From Cork they were taken to Bristol and, after being publicly sold in the market there, they were thrust on board ship, and borne to their final destination. The mind shrinks from imagining the horrors of their suffering at sea. From the records of survivors, they must have been at least equal to any of the sufferings experienced by African slaves on the way to America.

But, as certainly did not happen in the case of the latter, their hardships excited no sympathy in England. The inhabitants of Bristol watched them being packed on board and driven below with the same dull curiosity and phlegm, which they displayed in watching the embarkation of cattle. To them, doubtless, there was little to choose between a cow and an Irish Roman Catholic—neither, in their opinion, could feel sorrow or pain. In this manner did Oliver Cromwell ply his white slave traffic.

This order for the capture of Irish women was revoked after four years because it was found that the "man-catchers" had begun picking up even English women and girls in Ireland.

The following is quoted by John Patrick Prendergast in his *The Cromwellian Settlement of Ireland* (1865): "But at last the evil became too shocking and notorious, particularly when these dealers in Irish flesh began to seize the daughters and children of the English themselves, and to force them on board their slave ships; then indeed, the orders, at the end of four years, were revoked."

Cardinal Rinuccini had returned to Rome before the

debacle in Ireland. Nevertheless, he kept up a correspondence with some of the clergy who, in disguise, watched the wretched Irish slaves being forced aboard the slave ships.

> Nothing is more painful than to witness the shipment of those exiles, the father separated from his child, brother from brother, sister from sister, relative from relative, friend from friend, spouse from spouse . . . At one place we see the sons of noble families, the hope and consolation of their aged parents, youths delicately reared and carefully educated, who are not only robbed of every chance of their hereditary property, but are even despoiled of their more valuable clothes, receiving instead tattered rags, and are flogged with rods, and branded like sheep on their skin and flesh, and then driven among a crowd on board these infamous transportation ships.

We cannot today imagine the terror which must have been felt by the Irish at their first sight of the slave ships.

For most of the first half of the seventeenth century, the English slave trade was in the hands of privileged companies. The Company of Royal Adventurers, headed by the Duke of York and including a number of prominent courtiers, was founded in 1660. Even prior to that only very wealthy and influential people took part in the trade. For instance, the Company of Adventurers of London, which obtained a ten-year contract in 1618, was made up of prominent merchants. It took money to build and outfit ships, recruit crews and organise "goods", as the slaves were called, on the African side. The Bristol merchants had an advantage over other English ports. They were first in the tobacco trade, then in the indigo trade and, when that failed, the slave trade.

The slave ships, designed by the builders for the African trade, had specially designed holds. Shelves were fitted below decks, which doubled the number of people a ship could carry. The shelves allowed the slaves only two feet headroom, which meant that they could never sit up. As a certain Captain Newton, who was himself engaged in the African slave trade, put it, they were tightly packed "in two rows one above the other, on each side of the ship, close to each other like books upon a shelf. I have known them so close that the shelf would not easily contain one more . . . And I have known a man sent down among them to lay them in these rows to the greatest advantage, so that as little space as possible be lost." He adds, "and every morning perhaps more instances than one are found of the living and the dead fastened together".

The slaves were manacled two by two with iron shackles welded around the ankles. It meant that if one slave needed to use the stinking buckets, which were the only means of relieving the wants of nature, he had to drag his fellow slave with him.

On the African slave ships captains were known as "loose packers" or "tight packers". The tight packers held that the more they crammed into their ships, the more profit they made even thought the death rate would be higher. The loose packers, on the other hand, claimed that allowing the slaves that bit more room meant a lower death rate, and therefore it was more profitable to transport their slaves in that way. Captains received a bonus for every "piece of merchandise" that they landed safely in Barbados; it had nothing to do with being more humane. In the middle of the seventeenth century, it was usual to carry at least two slaves for each ton of the ship's weight, but very often a ship weighing 100 tons carried 250 slaves.

Some of the captains of these ships were brutes, having clawed their way up from able seamen to mates and then captains. It made no difference to them that their "cargo" was Irish and African slaves. They regarded them as goods for which they could obtain a good price on the Bridgetown markets. The men were even worse than their masters: seamen who had jumped ship, deserters from the

Royal Navy, men who had been shanghaied from the grog shops of Bristol, Liverpool and London, criminals who had escaped from gaols; in short, the scum of the earth.

We shall never know the exact number of Irish men, women and children transported to the living hell of the West Indies and the Americas. The numbers vary from as low as 12,000 by R.F. Foster, in *Modern Ireland* (1988), to 50,000 a year, which was the figure given by Cardinal Rinuccini, who described the desperate plight of the Irish put aboard the slave ships.

The Reverend Father Thomas Quyn, SJ, who somehow managed to avoid capture and transportation, wrote a report in Latin to Rome entitled "The State and Condition of Irish Catholics from the Year 1652–1656". It stated in part:

> And so these heretics [the English] caused the poor Catholics to be sent in crowded ships to Barbados and the Islands of America, such that those that did not die in the open remained in perpetual servitude. I believe that some 60,000 were sent there; the husbands expelled first to Spain and the Netherlands, whilst the wives and offspring were destined for America, such that there was a perpetual divorce; thus what God and nature had joined, the barbarous tyranny of the heretics separated.

According to the Reverend T.N. Burke in his series of lectures and sermons published in the New York's *Irish American* in the last century, some 80,000 to 100,000 "men of Ireland" were driven south to the ports of Munster where they were shipped to the sugar plantations of Barbados. Reverend Aubrey Gwynn, a historian who in the 1930s carried out considerable research of the period and who published his findings in a paper, "Cromwell's Policy of Transportation", thought this figure was an exaggeration. He came to the conclusion that probably 50,000 in all were transported in the five years between 1652 and 1657.

I am inclined to agree with Father Gwynn for several reasons: firstly, the relatives of the 34,000 (or 40,000 as some historians would have it) soldiers who were allowed to go abroad to join foreign armies were all later transported; secondly, there were the widows and orphans of soldiers killed in the eleven years war, between 1641 and 1652; thirdly, there were the vagrants and vagabonds, wanderers with no fixed abode. If Lord Broghill could boast that he could pick up 250 of them in a short period of time within a radius of twenty miles of Cork alone, how many more were picked up all over the country? Add to that number the Tories and priests, and in the whole of the Cromwellian period this figure could easily have reached 50,000, if not more. Of course, 50,000 or 60,000 was a drop in the ocean compared to the eleven million African slaves torn from their own countries and transported across thousands of miles to work on the sugar plantations of Barbados or the tobacco plantations of America, but a slave is a slave, no matter what the colour of the skin.

Not all of those put aboard the slave ships arrived at their destinations. For the slavers a loss of 20 per cent was acceptable, meaning that at least 10,000 died at sea of malnutrition, the rigors of the voyage or of various diseases. As Colonel A.B. Ellis' article in the *Argosy* magazine (1883) put it: "[I]t appears from the best information which is at present accessible that more than one-fifth of those who were shipped were flung to the sharks before the end of the voyage."

For the Bristol merchants the Irish slave trade was a better investment. The Irish white slaves cost about £4. 10s. a head, and they could be sold in Barbados for any sum between £10 and £35. Allowing for the death rate, the slaves on a 250-ton ship, tightly packed, could fetch a profit of almost £5000. This was much more lucrative than the triangular voyage: England–West Africa–Barbados. This passage often took up to twelve months as compared to the nine to twelve weeks that the voyage from Ireland to

Barbados took. Although the African slaves cost only the equivalent of £3 worth of goods a head, the length of the voyage, the death rate among the crew and the long wait in African ports to make up the cargo of black slaves cut into the profits.

These slave ships carried a larger and better paid crew than did ordinary cargo ships; some of the larger ones, those of 250 tons, carried crews of sixty or even seventy men. They were heavily armed with cannon and carronades (which fired partridge-shot) on the bow and aft decks and had a plentiful supply of muskets and cutlasses in case of mutinies aboard. Two members of the crew performed functions peculiar to slave ships. A carpenter was responsible, not only for the ordinary ship repairs, but for the erecting of benches between deck and hold to give extra space where slaves could be crammed and for erecting partitions separating the men from the women. The blacksmith, a second essential member of the crew of a slaver, was responsible for the leg irons, shackles, neck collars and chains.

As there is no record of how the Irish on the slave ships were treated (none ever returned), we have to assume that they were treated exactly as the African slaves were treated, for which there are many records. The ships usually put in at Vera Cruz to take on fresh supplies, and during this time the slaves were again confined to the holds with the hatches secured to prevent any attempt at escape or mutiny. It often took two or three days to take on supplies and to repair any damage caused by storms. While below the decks the slaves were fed by buckets of food being lowered down to them.

When the ships left Vera Cruz for the long haul to Barbados, the slaves were allowed up on deck more often. The crews of these ships did not have to contend with one problem which they had with Negro slaves: the Irish did not attempt suicide by jumping overboard or starving themselves to death, simply because their religion forbade it. Mutiny was a different factor; each time the slaves were allowed up on deck, the carronades were trained inboard and the gunners stood by with lighted matches. We have no direct evidence that mutinies occurred, but considering the various uprisings and rebellions in which the Irish undoubtedly took part during their slave years on the island, it is inconceivable that no show of resistance took place on board ship.

CHAPTER SEVEN

The Slavery of Sugar

"... *several were hanged; a great many 'sent to Barbadoes'* ...
A terrible Protector this. . . *He dislikes shedding blood, but is
very apt 'to Barbadoes' an unruly man—he sent and sends us
by the hundreds to Barbadoes, so that we have made an active
verb of it: 'Barbadoes you'.*"
A letter of 11 March 1655, concerning the Salisbury uprising
at the end of 1654

BARBADOS HAD CHANGED dramatically in the period
between the arrival of the Irish indentured servants
and the arrival of the first white slaves. It was no
longer the "Tobacco Island" mentioned by the
Clonmacnoise clergy. Barbadian tobacco became impossible to sell on the English market due to the superior qual-
ity of the Virginian crop. One contemporary writer called
its taste "earthy", and another noted that the planters did
not know how to cure it properly and described it as "the
worst that grows in the world".

With their tobacco unsaleable, the planters then turned
to growing cotton. The rich soil was perfectly suited for
this crop and for a time it was a success, but the bottom fell
out of the cotton market in 1640 when a glut of cotton
made it unprofitable to grow and ship it to England. They

then tried indigo, but the market for this was relatively small. It was at this crucial period in the island's history that sugar production began.

The history of sugar in the Caribbean is also the history of slavery and oppression on a scale that Europe had never known. It is a history of great fortunes amassed by white colonists from Europe and the enslavement of millions during its boom years in the Caribbean. It began with the introduction of the sugar cane plant by Columbus from the Canary Islands to Hispaniola. The soil proved suitable for the growing of sugar cane, and in 1516 the first sugar mill was established there. Two years later, a contemporary account described "fields of sugar cane that are wonderful to see, the cane as thick as a man's wrist and as tall as the height of two men of medium stature". Called by the Spaniards a *trapiche*, the first sugar mill was powered by horses that turned a wheel by moving steadily around a machine. If horses or oxen were not available, slaves were used. Later, Jews in Brazil invented a water-powered mill which the Spaniards called an *ingenio*, which produced twice as much sugar as the *trapiche*. This method of producing sugar had one drawback; it was confined to areas with plenty of water.

The cultivation of sugar cane spread to the English and French colonies in the Caribbean. Sugar is a labour-intensive industry and the Dutch, who had captured a part of Brazil from the Portuguese, were able to supply that labour. They had plenty of capital; Amsterdam was as important as London was in raising capital in the mid-seventeenth century, but the merchants there tended to prefer the certain profit from trade to the uncertain one from colonisation. Accordingly, thirty years later, when the Portuguese reoccupied Brazil and expelled the Dutch Jews, many moved to Barbados where they invested their capital in the sugar industry and the slave trade.

In 1690 Dalby Thomas, a historian, described the Dutch as mostly Jews and "external promoters in search of a moderate gain by trade". They saw the potential of Barbados as a market for slaves and sugar making machinery. Financing the sugar planters on the island would create a derivative demand for slaves. The Dutch had no real interest in indentured servants as a dominant system of labour organisation on the island, although they had engaged in the indentured service trade from Ireland in the 1630s, as we have seen in Captain West's narrative (Chapter Five). The leading position of the Dutch in the slave trade meant that they saw indentured servitude as inimical to their New World economic and social interests. Besides, being Jewish, the Dutch merchants who ended up in Barbados were not allowed by law to employ English servants themselves. Neither were they allowed to buy the indentures of early settlers, nor later of Irish or other white slaves. They were allowed only African slaves.

Sugar cane had been introduced to Barbados by a Dutchman in 1637 but was grown at first simply as fodder for cattle and crushed to make a sweet drink for local use. The planters had no knowledge of how to turn the cane into sugar. Richard Ligon (1657) gave an account of the beginnings of the sugar revolution on the island. As cultivation started in 1642, his is an almost contemporary account of its introduction:

> [A]t the time we landed on this Island, which was in the beginning of September 1647, we were informed, partly by those Planters we found there, and partly by our own observations, that the great work of sugar-making, was but newly practised by the inhabitants there. Some of the most industrious men, having gotten Plants from Pernambock, a place in Brasill, and made tryall of them at the Barbadoes; and finding them to grow, they planted more and more, as they grew and multiplyed on the place, till they had such a considerable number, as they were worth the while to set up a very small Ingenio, and so make tryall what Sugar could be made upon that soyl. But,

the secrets of the work being not well understood, the
Sugars they made were very inconsiderable, and little
worth.

But about the time I left the Island, which was in
1650, they were much better'd; for then they had the
skill to know when the Canes were ripe, which was
not . . . they were grown greater proficients, both in
boyling and curing them, and had learnt the knowledge of making them white. . . but not so excellent as
those they make in Brasill, nor is theyr any likelyhood
they can ever make such.

As events have shown, Ligon was certainly wrong on
this last point; the sugar industry became not only the sta-
ple one in Barbados, but the island itself became known as
"the Sugar Island". However, Ligon was correct in fore-
seeing the expansion of the large plantation at the cost of
the smaller one: "I believe when the small plantations of
poor men's land, ten, twenty, or thirty acres, which are too
small to lay to sugar plantations, be bought up by great
men, and put into plantations of five, six or seven hundred
acres, that two-thirds of the island will be fit for plantations of sugar, which will make it one of the richest spotes
on earth under the sun." The transition to sugar growing
changed the face of Barbadian society. The small tobacco
planters were wiped out and large sugar plantations of
between 100 and 500 acres took over.

The Sephardic Jews brought their know-how of sugar
milling, their capital and their slaves with them to
Barbados. "Wherever they went they brought with them
their skills as businessmen and their experience as sugar
planters, refiners and brokers." They also brought with
them the machinery needed for sugar refining, and
advanced money on long credit to the planters to buy it.
They taught them the art of planting, harvesting and
milling, and most important of all, sold them their black
slaves, again either on long credit or against the first
refined sugar produced. Before the advent of sugar there

were only a few hundred black slaves on the island, pur-chased from Dutch slave traders.

It was during the early days of sugar planting that the sup-ply of indentured servants began to run out. Many who signed indentures in the early days of the colony had now finished their indentures and were free men and women. Others had died of cholera, smallpox or dysentery. The Civil War in England created a shortage of ships, and men who would normally have signed as indentured servants were caught up in the conflict. To ease the labour situation, the Dutch Jews, with their experience of transporting African slaves to Brazil, now turned to importing them to Barbados. However, the planters, in the early days of the sugar revolu-tion, found them intractable and difficult to train, particu-larly for work in the mills. They cried out for white labour.

Cromwell, through his victories in England, Wales, Scotland and Ireland, solved their problem by shipping prisoners of war to Barbados. This not only solved the problem of what to do with a potentially seditious popu-lation, but also earned money for the Commonwealth. These prisoners were not sent as indentured servants, but were sold in perpetuity to the sugar planters of Barbados. They became the first white slaves in relatively modern times, slaves in the true sense of the word, owned body and soul by their masters.

Colonel A.B. Ellis, who did considerable research on the subject of white slaves, published his findings in a magazine named *Argosy* in 1883. In an article entitled "White Slaves and Bondservants in the Plantations", he wrote: "Few but readers of old Colonial papers and records, are aware that a lively trade was carried on between England and the Plantations as the Colonies were then called, from 1647 to 1690, in political prisoners, where they were sold to the Colonists for various terms of years, sometimes for Life."

Old records in the Barbados Museum and Historical Society files show that, according to planters' estimates, Barbados alone received thousands of prisoners of war who were regarded as white slaves. A survey carried out in 1650, even before the advent of the Irish white slaves there, showed that the island had a population of 20,000 white men. The first evidence we have of white men being sold is from Wales, where 240 Welsh "bachelors" were sold in May 1648 for a shilling each and shipped to Barbados. Ten thousand prisoners were taken at the battle of Worcester, mainly Scots with some German mercenaries. They were marched to London, and of those who survived, about 1500 were shipped to Barbados to be sold, presumably by auction, to the planters there.

A German soldier of fortune, Heinrich Von Uchteritz, gave an account of conditions there. He mucked out pig houses, swept out slave quarters, which he described as the most demeaning job for any white man, and worked in the cane fields under a sweltering sun for twelve hours a day, with an hour's break for a lunch of boiled maize. Von Uchteritz was lucky; after eighteen months of sweated labour, he was ransomed by some German merchants for 800 pounds of sugar and returned to Germany, where he wrote an account of his sufferings. Nothing further is known of the nineteen fellow German mercenaries captured with him. The Scots taken after Preston and Dunbar shared the same fate, shipped out in crowded transports to work in the sugar cane fields or in the mills.

Perhaps the most telling of all the evidence that these men were regarded as slaves comes in a statement of men taken during the Penruddock rising in 1655. The writers were Marcellus Rivers and Oxenbridge Foyle, on behalf of themselves and "three score and ten more Freeborn Englishmen". It was printed in "the eleventh year of England's liberty 1659", and begins: "The humble petition of Marcellus Rivers and Oxenbridge Foyle Gentlemen, and of three score and ten people of this nation now in slavery, humbly sheweth that your distressed Petitioners and others became prisoners at Exeter and Illchester in the west, upon pretence of the Salisbury Rising in the end of the year

1654, although many of them never saw Salisbury, or bore arms in their lives."

Having been in prison for over a year without trial, the statement continues, "they were hurried to Plymouth aboard the ship 'John of London', Captain John Cole, Master, where, after they had lain on shipboard fourteen days, the Captain hoisted sale, and at the end of the five weeks and four days anchored at the Isle of Barbados". It was an amazingly swift crossing for the period when most ships took between eight and ten weeks. They were transported in appalling conditions "kept lockt under decks amongst horses". On their arrival in May 1656, the master of the ship "sold your miserable petitioners to most inhumane and barbarous persons for 1,550 pounds weight of sugar apiece as the goods and chattels of Martin Noell and Major Thomas Alderyne of London". The petition goes on that those sold "were the aged of three score and seven years old, Divines, officers and Gentlemen". They were marched to the plantations where they endured "the most unsupportable captivity, grinding at the mills, attending the furnaces, or digging in the scorching Island, having nothing to feed on (notwithstanding their hard labour) but potato roots, nor anything to drink but water".

The petition continues to describe their treatment by their "Christian" masters, as "being bought and sold from one planter to another, or attached as horses and beasts for the debts of their masters, being whipt at the whipping post, as Rouges for their master's pleasure, and sleep in styes worse than hogs in England, and many other ways made miserable beyond expression or Christian imagination".

Another accompanying letter sent at the same time to the chief justice of the High Court reads: "My Noble Lord, I beg your Lordship's pardon for the rude approach by a slave, one of those many mentioned in the Slave Petition to Parliament, thrown together out of this sometime free and noble nation of England, and obscenely buried alive in the desolate vault, the Protestant Purgatory, Barbados."

Their petition led to a heated debate in Parliament on 25 March 1659. One member, Sir Arthur Haselrigge, said that "if we have fought our sons into slavery we are of all men most miserable".

Another member, Mr Boscowen, pointed out that, if such conditions were allowed to prevail "our lives will be cheap as those of Negroes... I would have you consider the trade of buying and selling men."

Martin Noell, planter and slaver, to whom Rivers and the others had been sold, had been elected MP for Staffordshire in 1656. He now intervened in the debate to assure the House that conditions on the plantations were not as bad as the petitioners alleged; that the servants (as he called them) were better off than the common husbandmen in England; and that Barbados was "a place as grateful to you for trade as any part of the world . . . not as odious as it is represented".

The speaker of the House, Sir William Lenthall, responding to the evidence, said, "I hope it is not the effect of war to make merchandise of our own men."

There are no records extant to show if Rivers, Foyle and the other gentlemen were ever repatriated, but at least they were able to draw the attention of the English public to the question of white slavery in Barbados.

In view of the above, it is surprising that some historians and authors deny that white slavery ever existed in Barbados. For instance, Michael Craton, in his *Sinews of Empire* (1974), states that there is absolutely no evidence that whites were ever true slaves in the English colonies. He goes on to quote Eric Williams, who in his *Capitalism and Slavery* (1942) states that whites were never quite slaves in the sense that blacks were. However, Craton does admit that the unfortunate Irish captives and perhaps some Barbadoed criminals were servants for life without indentures. Just what the Irish captives endured as "servants" without indentures is described in the following chapters.

CHAPTER EIGHT

The Sugar Plantations

"Barbados was one of the Richest spotes of ground in the worlled where the gentry doeth live far better than ours doue in England."
Henry Whistler, *Journall of a Voyage* (1655)

MORE AND MORE settlers arrived from England to buy plantations. Richard Ligon describes a sugar plantation in 1648 which was bought by a friend of his, a Colonel Modyford. Modyford had taken part in the Civil War as a royalist officer at Exeter and, like many other royalists, sought refuge in Barbados. He arrived in the same ship as Ligon and bought a half share in this particular plantation. Ligon was his guest during his three-year period of stay on the island. Modyford, in the manner of the time, later changed his policies and went on to become governor of Jamaica under Cromwell. Ligon wrote of Modyford's plantation as containing:

> 500 acres of land, with a faire Dwelling House and Ingenio in a room 400 feet square, a boyling house, filling house, cisternes and still house, with a curing house 100 feet long and 40 feet broad, with stables and smith's forge and room to lay provisions of Corne and Banavist. Houses for Negroes and Indian

Slaves, with 96 Negroes and 3 Indian women with their children, 28 Christians, 45 cattle for work, 8 milch cows, a dozen horses and mares and 11 Assinigoes . . . In this plantation of 500 acres, there was employed for sugar something more than 200 acres, about 80 acres for pasture, 120 for wood, 20 for Tobacco, 5 for Ginger, as many for Cotton Wool, 70 acres for provisions, viz, corne, potatoes, Plantaines, Cassavie and Banavist; some few acres of which were for fruit, viz. Pines, Plantaines, Millions, Bonanas, Goaves, Water Millions, Oranges and Limons.

Modyford paid £7000 for his half share. Eight years earlier the whole estate had been worth only £400. Unlike most other plantations of its size, Modyford's seems to have had only a small number of African slaves. Plantations of this size usually had at least 150 to 200 slaves working on them. The "28 Christians" were probably indentured servants, as no white slaves had reached Barbados during Ligon's stay there.

As the cultivation of sugar increased, so did the number of black slaves. In Barbados there were only a couple of hundred in 1640, but by 1646 there were 6000 blacks and about 40,000 whites, including indentured servants. Fourteen years later there were 46,000 blacks and only 20,000 whites. The decline in the number of whites may be attributed to several factors, the main one being the squeezing out of the small tobacco grower, whose plantation of twenty-five, thirty or thirty-five acres was absorbed into the larger sugar estates. The white owner of the small holding who was not willing to work as an employee of a rich planter had to seek a living in one of the other islands or to return to England.

The sugar revolution began almost at the same time as the Civil War in England. Royalists, who had their estates confiscated, fled to the island, bringing what capital they could lay their hands on. Many Roundheads, those who were originally parliamentarians but did not agree with the execution of Charles I, also came to Barbados and bought property. These new settlers, particularly the royalists, were a different breed of men from the pioneers. Some had been at court and others had lived in lavish style on their estates in England. Most had led profligate lives; gamblers, rakes, womanisers and heavy drinkers, they saw no reason to change their lifestyle when they reached Barbados. In 1644, forty-six of the new settlers held estates of over 500 acres apiece.

The Roundheads seemed to lay their political affiliations aside on their arrival. Ligon noted that although the colonists were of different religious and political background, they were able to transcend the cleavage and achieve unity for the common exploitation of colonial resources: "They were loving, friendly and hospitable one to another and although they were of different persuasions, yet their descretions ordered everything so well that there was never any falling out between them." It was considered a breach of good manners to call anyone a Cavalier or a Roundhead. The offender was condemned to give a turkey dinner to which all his neighbours, Cavalier and Roundhead, were invited.

The Earl of Clarendon wrote of the fortunes that could be made in Barbados by relatively poor men when they went into sugar planting. For example, one such planter, a Colonel James Drax, became one of the richest and most influential men on the island, ending up with a knighthood and marrying the Earl of Carlisle's daughter. According to Ligon his "beginning upon that Island was founded [on] a stock not exceeding 300 pound sterling, has raised his fortune to such a height, as I have heard him say, that he would not look towards England, with the purpose to remaine there the rest of his life, till he were able to purchase an estate of tenne thousand pounds land yearly, which he hoped in few years to accomplish, with what he was then owner of; and all by this plant of Sugar".

Another man who rose from small beginnings was a Thomas Rous. He arrived in Barbados in 1638 in an over-crowded ship holding 350 passengers, of whom two thirds were indentured servants. On his arrival he was given sixty acres, but when the tobacco crop failed, sold out for £720. However, when sugar was introduced, he bought back his plot and from then on must have acquired other holdings, as by 1680 his son, John, was shown as owning 658 acres, three sugar mills, seven white servants and 340 slaves.

The governor of Barbados during its transition from tobacco to sugar was Sir Philip Bell, who had much experience in the colonies as he had at one time been governor of Bermuda. He was an able man and during his period of office developed a judicial system, set up the Church of England as the established church, reorganised the militia, and gave the elected Council of Barbados the power to pass laws as it saw fit. During his time as governor he made attendance at divine service on Sundays compulsory and ordered officials to "search taverns, alehouses, victualling houses, or other houses, where they doe suspect lewd and debauched company to frequent".

Under Bell Barbados was a peaceful place. The Earl of Clarendon wrote of it: "The Barbadoes, which was much the richest plantation, was principally inhabited by men who had retired thither only to be quiet, and to be free from the noise and oppressions in England, and without any ill thoughts towards the King; many of them having served him with fidelity and courage during the war; and, that being ended, made that island their refuge from further prosecutions."

The peace of the island was rudely disturbed by the arrival of Lord Willoughby on 30 April 1650, bearing a commission from Charles II appointing him governor of Barbados. He immediately deposed Bell and became the principal cause of the split between the local royalists and parliamentarians.

Neither Cromwell nor Parliament could ignore this

challenge to their authority. A force was assembled to attack and take the island. The mobilisation took some time, and it was not until 5 August 1651 that it was ready to sail. The squadron consisted of seven war ships and six merchantmen under the command of Cromwell's old friend, Sir George Ayscue, who had sailed down the east coast of Ireland and had helped Cromwell in the taking of Wexford. It was a weak force of only 1000 men, but Ayscue intended to starve the island into submission rather than take it by force of arms.

On arrival he sent a demand for the island's surrender "for the use of the Parliament of England". To this Willoughby replied that he acknowledged "no supreme authority over Englishmen but the King, and by his Commission; and for him I do, and by God's assistance shall, defend this place". The Council and Assembly of Barbados also issued a joint declaration: "That we will, with ye uttmost hazard to our Lives and fortunes defend His Majesty's Interest and Lawfull Power in and to this Island." This document was signed by, among others, Colonel Modyford and Henry Hawley. When Modyford later changed his mind and threatened to go over to the parliamentarians, Willoughby had no option but to surrender. An agreement was signed between Willoughby and Ayscue, which was called the Charter of Barbados.

This was a remarkable document, in that it contained provisions for an act of indemnity, giving immunity to everyone concerned in opposition to the parliamentary forces, and allowing the Council and Assembly to function as hitherto, with the sole provision that the governor would be appointed from England. Daniel Searle took over the post. Although the planters were forced to accept the terms of the charter, many objected to Searle's being made governor, arguing that since corporations in England elected their chief magistrates, colonial communities should have the same privilege. Searle reported to Parliament that although the people had submitted they had not done so willingly; that they were restless spirits, unsatisfied with the constitution of England and that they would like to make "this little limb of the Commonwealth into a free state".

When things had returned to normal after the turbulent events of what became known in England as "the Horrid Rebellion", sugar production went on apace. A planter elite grew up, and by the middle of the seventeenth century it was firmly entrenched in the colony's political and legal institutions.

Composed largely of English gentry and merchants, they dominated Barbadian life in every way. They held ten out of the twelve seats in the island's Council, twenty of the twenty-two seats in the Assembly, and were nineteen out of the twenty-three judges. The planters lived in big houses, built like fortifications in case of slave uprisings. They ate off gold plate, dressed in the latest London fashion, and according to Ligon were "attended by bewigged butlers, pages, coachmen and postillions, while the humbler parts of the mansion swarmed with a retinue of cooks, washers, waiters, stable boys and maids". He goes on to describe their life style: "[T]hey lived in a feudal style with grand houses, balls, etc. Many lived beyond their means, with fine furniture, gold plate, coaches and packs of hounds. They over eat and over drink and spend much time in horse racing, gambling etc."

Large plantations were now the norm, owned by men such as Newton, Codrington, Modyford, Skeete, Berringer, Waldron, Drax and the Noell brothers. Most of the houses were built of wood of which there was a plentiful supply, although one, St Nicholas Abbey, owned by Benjamin Berringer, was constructed of stone and still stands today with few modifications.

Colonel John Scott, a visitor to the island who wrote a long description of his experiences there, described black and white slaves working together in the fields: "[They] are just permitted to live, and a very great part Irish, derided by the Negroes and branded with the Epithet of white slaves... I have for my particular satisfaction inspected many [of] their Plantations, and have seene 30; sometimes 40, Christians, English, Scotch and Irish at worke in the parching sun without shirt, shoe or stocking." A French priest, Père Labat, who visited Barbados in 1700, also referred to some field workers as "white slaves".

Slaves were divided into two main classes: the field slaves and the house slaves. There were four categories of both black and white field slaves, divided according to their age and strength, each with a specific task.

The number one or "great gang" was composed of strong, mature black and white men and women for actual field operations. They performed the hardest work on the plantations. During crop time, from February to April or early May, more hours of continuous labour were required than at any other time. The great gangs, driven by whips, often worked a twenty-hour day, but received extra food during this period. They worked without their mid-morning break and were allowed one hour for their dinner. They cut the cane and carried it to the mills that produced the sugar. During the out of crop season, the great gang was occupied in tilling the fields, digging cane holes, planting canes and food crops, and collecting animal dung and human excrement which was then taken by them to the fields and used as fertiliser.

The second gang, called the "little gang", was composed of adolescents with an average age of around fifteen. They weeded the fields, planted food crops such as corn, and during the season gathered cane trash for sugar-factory fuel. The cane trash was also used as thatching material for the slave huts.

The third gang was made up of children from the ages of five or six years up to eleven or twelve. They were called the "meat pickers gang" or the "hog minders gang", and their main job was to collect grass or fodder for the animals. They also attended to the fowls and small animals, and made up about 15 per cent of the total slave population.

The fourth gang was made up of those who performed skilled work on the plantations: carpenters, masons, coopers, potters, etc. Picked men of this gang worked also in the sugar mills, feeding the cane into the mill's rollers, or working as distillers, boilers, clayers and clarifiers. The head boiler was a highly skilled man, one of the most important of all the slaves on the plantation. He had his own hut set apart from the other slaves' quarters and was fed much better than any of the others. William Dickson, who lived in Barbados for thirteen years at the beginning of the eighteenth century, observed that members of the fourth gang lived in comparative ease, both in town and country; nor could they be said to feel any of the hardships of slavery, but such as arose from the caprices of their owners, which were intolerable enough.

Life on a plantation was a continuous round of labour under the blistering sun and drenching rain. The hardest part of the work was when the slaves began the preparation of the land for the cultivation of the young shoots of the sugar cane. The ground was readied for planting with no other tool than the hoe; there were few ploughs in Barbados during the seventeenth century, and they were only introduced in any numbers in the mid-eighteenth. The young canes were planted in November in holes ten inches deep and two feet apart. This might involve shifting up to twelve cubic feet of earth and the digging of eighty holes, which was a hard day's work, although this was the minimum expected. About 3000 holes were dug for every acre. Cane cuttings from neighbouring fields were then placed in each hole and covered with several inches of mould. When the young shoots began to appear, more mould was added, and all the time the greatest care had to be taken in clearing the weeds. After about sixteen months the canes were ready for cutting. This took place between February and May and was the busiest time on any plantation. All hands were mobilised to assist in the work. Slaves, blacks and whites, often worked far into the night when harvesting began, as the backbreaking task of cutting the cane had to be performed in a short time to prevent over-ripening. The cane was cut with cutlasses or machetes, and the work was not only hard but also called for considerable skill. They had to be cut low on the stems, which were very tough, and the greatest care had to be exercised not to damage the bud from which the ratoons (the new shoots) would spring the following year.

The canes were loaded on to carts drawn by donkeys or slaves and unloaded at the sugar mill. This factory-like structure was situated in the middle of the cane fields. The work in the mill called for strength and skill, and the men worked long shifts, day and night, maintaining the boiling houses. Here the canes were crushed on huge rollers, powered either by oxen or slaves, and the juice was run off into vats below. The extracted juice was then taken to the boiling house. There it was poured into a series of copper vats which were kept constantly boiling. The fire in the open oven had to be tended day and night, and the various pots had to be kept at an even temperature so that all impurities could be removed. This job required special skills in feeding and damping the fire underneath each vat, and was usually carried out by the white slaves. The men working in the boiling house became so debilitated that their resistance to pulmonary disease and the many epidemics that swept the island was lowered, and the death rate among them was particularly high. After a few days when the sugar crystals formed, wet clay was placed on this mixture, and this seeped through and separated the sugar crystals from the molasses. The vats were removed to the cooling house, where the sugar was bagged and kept in storage rooms until it was ready to be transported to the docks to await shipment to England.

As with the indentured servants, conditions for the slaves on the sugar plantations varied according to the character of the master, particularly with regard to the supply of food. Some masters not alone supplied food in reasonable quantities but also allowed slaves to grow yams, peas, sweet potatoes, cassava, melons, cucumber and pumpkins on small plots of land which were set aside for them. The best rations went to the sugar boilers, usually white men. Their skill in making the sugar determined whether the estate made a profit or not, so the master spared neither food nor drink for them. However, Père Labat wrote, "The English do not look after their slaves well, and treat them very badly."

The growing and milling of sugar cane, although a lucrative enterprise, was subject to certain set-backs. One of these was the weather. From the very beginning of the settlement of Barbados, hurricanes were a frequent occurrence, but they were disastrous when the growing of sugar canes began. They uprooted whole fields, destroyed the mills and boiling houses and not infrequently damaged the great houses, many of which at the time were wooden buildings. They swept away the flimsy huts of the slaves and left them open to the elements. Adding to the misery of the slaves, in particular those whose huts were destroyed, the incessant lightning must have been terrifying in the exposed terrain. Slaves would lose everything, including often their lives, as their quarters were usually built on low-lying land in areas which became raging torrents. There are many records in the State Papers (Colonial) of such hurricanes. For instance, there was a petition presented to the Council of State on 18 November 1656 on behalf of Martin Noell and ten of the leading planters, merchants and traders of Barbados to the Lord Protector in Council which stated: "having received intelligence that the recent extraordinary rains lately fallen on the island, their horses, cattle, Negroes and other servants were destroyed and their works must lie still until they be supplied". They asked for licences to export 600 horses and 600 cattle. This was endorsed by the Lord Protector the same day.

No mention is made here of the replacement of slaves; as Martin Noell was one of the principal dealers in both black and white slaves, those lost were speedily replaced. The flimsy huts of the slaves were reconstructed as soon as the ground dried out. It says much for the resilience of the planters and merchants of Barbados that within twelve months their homes and shops would be rebuilt, and life carried on as before. However, the damage to the sugar cane fields was more serious, as during a violent storm, which usually occurred during the months of July to October, crops and sugar mills could be damaged so severely that an entire season's crop would be lost.

The second hurricane of which we have a particular record occurred on the 10 October 1780 and is referred to as "the Great Hurricane". It caused thousands of deaths and did immense damage to property on the island and ships in the harbour. We have an account of it by Admiral Rodney, who arrived in Barbados some weeks after the hurricane had struck: "The whole Face of the Country appears an entire ruin, and the most Beautiful Island in the World has the appearance of a country laid waste by fire and Sword, and appears to the Imagination more Dreadful that it is possible for me to find Words to express."

The vagaries of the climate, the diseases of the island and the difficulties of managing a plantation made the chance to retire and buy an estate in England and live in comfort for the rest of their lives an ambition of many planters. Most married planters were loath to bring their wives and families to Barbados because of the many endemic diseases and the lack of skilled medical attention. There was also the problem of education for their children and the lack of any culture or entertainment. Added to that was the sense of insecurity, brought about by living in close proximity to a slave society based entirely on coercion. The docile slave of today could become the crazed killer of tomorrow. A constant vigilance was required, whether in the home or in the fields, and, for some at least, the daily witnessing of slaves under punishment of the lash proved too much.

The absentee landlords cared nothing for the good of the island or for their civic duty in defending it. All they wanted was the profits their sugar estates could yield, and to get the maximum revenue they put their lands into the hands of white overseers, men who had come out of England but had not had enough money to buy their own land. Many hoped, eventually, to make enough to buy an estate, and to that end they treated their slaves unmercifully, squeezing the last ounce of work out of them. They were not socially accepted by the resident planters and spent all their time on the plantations, often with five or six slave mistresses. They remitted the profits demanded by the absentee landlords, many of whom never set foot in Barbados again.

The absentee landlords in England were a strong force who exercised a considerable influence at court and later in the Council for Trade and Plantations. They were able to exert strong pressure on the selection of governors for the various colonies. In 1677 Sir Jonathan Atkins, then governor of Barbados, complained that the Lords of Trade and Plantation took the advice of absentee landlords in England rather than the man on the spot. In turn, the planters living in Barbados complained to the Council and referred to the opposition of some governors, claiming that there was no liberty left in Barbados. They mentioned the case of one governor who had a speaker of the Assembly publicly whipped through the streets of Bridgetown.

The Assembly frequently complained of the ill effects of absenteeism on the public service of the island. An agent for Barbados in England wrote in 1689: "By a kind of magnetic force, England draws to it all that is good in the plantations. It is the centre to which all things tend. Nothing but England can we relish or fancy: our hearts are here, where ever our bodies be. If we get a little money, we remit it to England. Where we are a little easy, we desire to live and spend what we have in England. And all that we can reap and rend is brought to England."

The prince of absentees was a William Beckford of Jamaica, who built the imposing county seat Fonthill Splendens in Wiltshire. Beckford and his three brothers had seats in Parliament and he became an alderman of the city of London and a lord mayor. He defended absenteeism on the ground that "the climate of our sugar colonies is so inconvenient for an English constitution, that no man will choose to live there".

If the planters in Barbados or Jamaica were forced by circumstances to remain on the island, they sent their children to England to be educated. The establishment of schools on both of these islands was neglected. "Learning is here at the lowest ebb," wrote a historian of Jamaica in 1740. "There is no public school in the whole island, neither do they seem fond of the thing; several large donations have been made for such uses but have never taken effect. The office of a teacher is looked upon as contemptible . . . A man of any parts or learning that would employ himself in that business would be despised and starve."

Many of the rich planters kept their wives in England and consequently took the black slaves as their mistresses. According to Eric Williams, in his book *From Columbus to Castro* (1972), this produced all gradations of miscegenation, which the planters produced from their game of "'washing their blackamoors white'—that is the planter slept with his daughter and his granddaughter and so on, through all the grades of incest". This was one of the reasons why the planters welcomed the Irish women. As Henry Cromwell wrote, they had only "Negro and Maroon women to solace them".

CHAPTER NINE

The Irish Via Dolorosa

*"Those sold to the heretics in America are treated by them
more cruelly than the slaves under the Turks; nor is any
attention paid to youth or the decrepitude of old age, to sex or
rank, to sacerdotal orders to religious life."*
Cardinal Giovanni Battista Rinuccini, papal nuncio to the
Confederation of Kilkenny (1645–48)

S LAVES CAN BE defined as persons who are the absolute
property of their masters for life. The slaves of
Barbados had no wills of their own, but were subject
to their masters' whims or caprices. They could be mortgaged, sold, gambled or given in payment of debts. They
could be flogged to death on the merest whim of their masters or mistresses, without the latter incurring any penalty,
or, at the most, a derisory fine of twenty shillings. The
progeny of slaves, when they were allowed to cohabit or
marry with their masters' consent, became the property of
their owners. This applied to both Irish and black slaves.

The courts were never open to either group of slaves
and, as has been shown, to very few indentured servants.
The greatest difference between the indentured servants
and the white slaves, however, lay in the one word—
HOPE. The servants knew that, no matter how appalling

their sufferings, the time must come when their indentures ended and they became free men and women. The white slaves had no such solace. They were slaves for life and their only release was in death.

By the time the first Irish white slaves arrived in Barbados, Bridgetown was a very different city from the shanty town it had been when the first Irish indentured servants reached it. It had become a typical seventeenth century seaport, with red tiled roofs, brick chimneys, wharves and quays, and its bay was full of ships riding at anchor. Père Labat described it thus: "The houses are well built in the English style with many glass windows; they are magnificently furnished. The shops and merchants' warehouses are filled with all one could wish from all parts of the world . . . one notices the opulence and good taste of the inhabitants in their magnificent furniture and silver of which they all have considerable quantities."

Colonel John Scott also described the opulence of the planters' houses: "In the year 1666 I found by a rationall Estimate, the plates, Jewells and extraordinary household stuffe to be worth about £200,000, and their buildings very faire and beautiful."

When the ships carrying the Irish slaves docked at Bridgetown, factors went aboard to assess the cargo. The slaves were allowed four days in which to recover from the rigours of their voyage. Fresh food was brought on board and they were allowed a limited freedom to walk around the deck. The manacles were removed, but the leg irons remained in place. The men were given pipes and tobacco and a tot of rum each day. As with the African slaves, effort was made to make them look more presentable and therefore more saleable on the auction block. They were hosed down with seawater and deloused.

The slaves were divided into four categories: women and girls, men and boys, the children of both sexes and, lastly, the "refuse", those who were unfit for much labour or were too old or sick. The "refuse" was sold off first.

They were forced to stand on the auction block while the factor endeavoured to drum up interest in them. A large crowd of planters and seamen from other ships gathered to watch the proceedings. If the eighty-year-old Fitzgeralds of Lackagh Castle and others like them had survived the voyage, they would have been classed as "refuse" and undergone similar treatment. They were quickly disposed of at derisory prices, and then the real sales began.

First came the men and boys. Planters went among them, feeling their muscles and opening their mouths to judge their ages. When the women and girls appeared there was a visible stir of interest in the crowd. Like the African slaves, it is even possible that they were stripped before being put on the auction block. The older women were disposed of first, and the planters who required field labour went among them and, after an examination, bought them, often in batches. Then came the turn of the young Irish girls. These aroused the greatest interest, as the planters wanted them mainly as concubines or sexual playthings. Again the physical examination was a thorough one, the buyer often bringing a "churgeon" or a midwife to examine them and assure themselves that they were buying a virgin. The children, boys and girls, came last. They were dragged screaming on to the auction block where again they were vetted. The richer planters and their wives required the boys as pages and the young girls to be trained as maids or house servants. Occasionally they were bought for more sinister reasons. Homosexuals and paedophiles frequented these auctions, buying at inflated prices children whose fate would be years of debauchery until they became too old for such purposes and were then sold off to the numerous brothels in Bridgetown.

One further degradation awaited the slaves. A heated branding iron bearing their owner's initials was applied to the bare skin; in the case of women and girls to the forearm; in the case of men and boys to the buttocks. The slaves were then issued with cotton trousers and shirts for the men and gowns for the women, and driven, guarded by mulattos with cow-hide whips, to the plantations. Those who fell were flogged and then thrown into carts.

When they reached the plantation, there was no planter to meet them, no seniors to show them how to construct huts as had happened in the case of the indentured servants. As they were driven towards the slave lines, they may have caught a glimpse of the Big House as they entered the great iron gates, but for most of them that was all they ever saw of it.

The black slave lines were in a hollow, out of sight of the occupants of the Big House, and were built of sticks and plantain leaves. They were sparsely furnished, and the slaves slept on the ground on a bed of rushes, which were changed once a week. The only utensils were a wooden spoon and bowl. Their one meal a day consisted of maize, loblolly and sweet potatoes. To satisfy the wants of nature, a large trench was dug behind the lines and was used by men and women alike. During the rainy season it often overflowed, causing a stench which was guaranteed to turn the most hardened stomach. The Irish were dispersed among the black slaves, which, because they had no common language, lessened the danger of revolt. It must be remembered that at this juncture the majority of the Irish white slaves did not speak English and the commands of the overseers were incomprehensible to them. They were lost and bewildered in a strange world where only the fittest survived.

The slaves were put to work on the day following their arrival. The young women and girls had already been sent to the Big House for their master's sexual gratification or to be employed as maids or servants. The Reverend E.A. D'Alton (1910) described the segregation:

> The men and boys were put to work in the sugar
> plantations; the girls and women—wives and widows
> of officers and soldiers, gently nurtured perhaps, and
> in the manners refined—were to be the wives and

mistresses of the West Indian Planters to take the
place of negresses and maroons . . . Their beauty was
their ruin and attracted their master's lustful eyes
and, in that land of the tropics and the trade winds,
they lived as in a prison, their faith banned, their race
and nation despised, their virtue outraged, their tears
derided, and as they looked out on the waving fields
of sugar cane, they sadly thought of their own dear
land with its fields so fertile and so green, now separated from them forever by thousands of miles of
rolling sea.

A worse fate awaited some of the girls and women not
bought by the planters. There are records in the Public
Archives of Barbados of stud farms being set up by small
planters, who frequented every auction and bought up
likely looking "breeders". These white-slave merchants
had set up in business long before the Irish slaves arrived.
As early as 1638, they were buying the indentures of servant women and breeding from them. They were often the
fathers of white children of such a union, and when the
girls were old enough, at the age of twelve or thirteen, they
were sold to the madams of the brothels in Bridgetown,
brothels which catered for the local planters and the ships'
officers. When a girl had lost her looks, she was then resold
to a lower class brothel catering for ordinary seamen, usually run by mulatto women.

The records also show that these stud farms specialised
in mixed breeding. Coromantine and Mandingo men were
usually chosen as sires, for among all the African tribes
enslaved, they were considered to be the strongest and most
intelligent. Careful records were kept, much like the ones
they kept for their horses. A good breeder was an invalu-
able asset on such farms, but was worn out by her early
twenties, having had her first child at the age of twelve or
thirteen. The progeny of such unions, particularly the
females, were eagerly sought after by the local planters,
who found the Irish sexually cold and unresponsive, having

to be whipped into submission. The lightly coloured mulatto girls bred on the farms were, on the other hand, not only eager, but also trained for every kind of sexual proclivity. Many of them, therefore, fetched high prices in the brothels of Bridgetown, and some even ended up owning their own establishments. The mulatto boys were sold to homosexual planters or were given work as houseboys in the Big Houses.

It was a very profitable business for the small planter, as when the white women and black men were not engaged in procreation, they were used as slave labour in his fields or hired out to the owners of the large plantations as extra labour during harvest time. It was probably to this type of planter that William Dickson, who lived in Barbados for thirteen years towards the end of the seventeenth century, referred to when he wrote:

> Slavery corrupts the morals of the master, by freeing him from those restraints with respect to his slaves, so necessary for the control of human passions, so beneficial in promoting the practice and confirming the habit of virtue. It is dangerous to the master because his oppression excites implacable resentment in the slave and the extreme misery of his condition continually prompts him to risk the gratification of them and his situation daily furnishes the opportunity.

In 1665, Sir Thomas Modyford, referring to this type of planter and the general intemperance of the Barbadian and Jamaican population, spoke particularly of "old army officers, who from strict saints are turned the most debauched devils".

Of course the foregoing was not true of all planters, many of whom were decent, honourable men and treated their white and black slaves humanely. Some even married their Irish mistresses, and their sons and daughters were sent to good schools in England. It must be said that these marriages were rare. The planters were mainly Protestant, with a deep-rooted hatred of the Irish Catholics, whether indentured servants or slaves. By most of these planters, the Irish were regarded as lazy, shiftless, drunken, disobedient and recalcitrant; they were flogged more often than their Scots or English fellow slaves and regarded by the governor and the planters as treacherous and likely to join with their French or Spanish coreligionists in the event of an invasion. They were not even considered Christian by the Puritans. These were extreme Protestants of the sixteenth and seventeenth centuries, whose aim was the purification of religious practices from anything not specifically authorised by scripture and who enjoined the strictest purity of conduct. They certainly did not practise what they preached. Most of them in Barbados had mistresses and most owned white as well as black slaves.

Of the treatment of slaves on the plantations, William Dickson wrote:

> The great body of slaves, the field people on the plantations are generally treated more like beasts of burden than like human creatures, since they cultivate the land with no assistance from cattle, and suffer every hardship which can be supposed to attend to oppressive toil, coarse and scanty fare, bad lodgings, want of covering in the wet season, and a degree of severity which frequently borders on, and too often amounts to, inhumanity.

All the field slaves were called out at daybreak for their work by a blast on a horn. Those who were not on time were flogged. They worked in rows under the whips of drivers, who were mainly mulattos, a certain number of whom were allotted to each gang. The weak were forced to keep up with the strong. They worked from daylight to darkness with two intermissions, one for half an hour in the morning, the other for two hours at noon. The drivers or overseers made no distinction of sex in the use of the whip. If a pregnant woman was unable to keep up with the rest of the gang, the whip was applied without any regard for her condition. In some cases, to prevent the loss of a future slave through a miscarriage, a hole was dug in the earth into which the belly of the pregnant woman would fit while she was whipped.

For every slave, Irish or African, the ever-present whip was the symbol of the master's dominance and their status of degradation. On some of the plantations the newly bought slaves were flogged on their arrival simply to emphasise their present status and to inspire in them a terror of their masters and overseers. The overseers carried their whips at all times, some never removing them even at night. One boasted that he could take all the skin off a mule within fifteen minutes; another that he could decapitate a slave with one stroke at a distance of ten feet.

The whipping post was set in the centre of the slave compound and consisted of a single post driven into the ground with a crossbar at the top. The floggings usually took place at sunset when the slaves had returned from the fields but before they had dispersed to their huts. The man or woman sentenced to be whipped was stripped naked and the hands were tied to the crossbar, lifting the body so that the toes just touched the ground. The overseer then stood back, removed the whip from his belt, measured his distance and laid on the first blow. The second stroke criss-crossed the first, and so it went on until the victim fainted. A bucket of cold water, to which salt had been added, was thrown over the slave. When he or she regained consciousness the flogging continued. Vinegar, and at times pepper, were rubbed into the victim's wounds simply to increase the pain, and then the slave was cut down and carried to his or her hut. The master sometimes attended such floggings; they were intended as a lesson to the other slaves. It must be remembered that in those days whipping at the cart's tail through a town was a regular public spectacle, and flogging was a ritual punishment in the English army and navy. Women field workers were flogged in the same way as the men, but sometimes the overseer would use a lighter whip which did not inflict so much damage.

It was not only at the whipping post that the white slaves were flogged; from their very first days in the fields they would feel the driver's lash on their bare backs. Often these newcomers could not keep up with the experienced blacks at the field work, and for this the lash descended.

The mulatto drivers enjoyed using the whip on whites. It gave them a sense of power and was also a protest against their white sires. White women in particular were singled out for the punishment in the fields. Sometimes, to satisfy a perverted craving, the mulatto drivers forced the women to strip naked before commencing the flogging and then forced them to continue working all day under the blistering sun. While the women were weeding in the fields in that condition, the drivers often satisfied their lust by taking them from the rear.

Slaves, white and black, were sold or exchanged frequently. A special slave mart was held in Bridgetown every month, and there a planter could get rid of "sucklings" (young slaves), sell off some others and buy any number of new ones he required. Sales were by auction and were advertised beforehand. The slaves at such auctions were stripped, forced on to the auction block and after a thorough inspection, bought at an agreed price between the vendor and the buyer. Young slave girls, often only ten or eleven years old, were bought by the madams of brothels of Bridgetown, frequented by planters and seamen.

The white slaves working in the fields endured other torments. An overseer, if he so desired, could withhold water from them all day and then force them to crawl on their bellies to the cattle trough and there drink the muddied water. They had no recourse to anybody, no appeal. If the god-like master of the plantation did deign to ride among them, they had to lower their eyes. To look at him directly invoked a flogging. Even the slightest error in the fields, such as pulling up a ratoon instead of a weed, was punished by a whipping.

House servants were flogged by a man known as a "jumper", usually a lightly coloured mulatto. The method and instrument of punishment were slightly different. The slave was stripped and tied face down to a flat board and the instrument used was called a "paddle", which was a piece of wood shaped like a boat paddle, with the broad end covered with cowhide. The covered end measured about a foot across, narrowing down to a handle. The paddle was usually applied to the culprit's posterior and thighs. The blows did not break the skin, but raised large blisters. When the beating was over, the victim was expected to resume work immediately. The jumper's lot was not an enviable one, as the mistress of the house supervised the floggings, and if she thought that the jumper was not laying on the paddle hard enough, she belaboured him with her riding crop.

Another contemporary writer described some of the other punishments, such as gelding or chopping off half the foot with an axe. He added that:

> These Punishments are suffered by them with great Constancy: . . . For running away, they put Iron Rings of great weight on the Ankles, or Pottocks about their Necks, which are Iron Rings with two long Necks rivetted to them or a Spur in the Mouth. For Negligence, they are usually whipt by the Overseers with Lancewood Switches, till they be bloody, and several of the Switches broken . . . The Cicatrices are visible on their Skins for ever after; and a Slave, the more he have of those, is the less valu'd. After they are wip'd till they are Raw, some put on their Skins Pepper and Salt to make them smart; at other times their Masters will drop melted Wax on their Skins, and use several very exquisite Torments.

House servants were beaten for the slightest offence: not coming quickly enough to their master or mistress's call, breaking a cup or a plate, or for oversleeping when the first blast of the horn echoed through the estate. Richard Ligon described the case of two young daughters of a plantation owner who stripped a black slave girl, tied her hands and feet with their own garters, and beat her "almost to death" with the heels of their shoes. Her offence was dropping a china plate.

The ultimate penalty was hanging. If a slave attempted to strike a master or overseer, a court was quickly convened in Bridgetown. It usually consisted of three justices of the peace, all planters. The accused, who had been lodged in the Cage (the prison in Bridgetown), was brought before them in chains. It was simply a formality. He, or very occasionally she, was not allowed to say anything in his or her defence. After hearing the planter's or overseer's statement, the sentence was almost invariably death by hanging. The slave was hanged in public before a large crowd. When the body was lowered, the head was cut off and given to the planter, who mounted it on a high pole in the slaves' quarters as a macabre warning to the others.

CHAPTER TEN

Revolts and Rebellions

> *"Whereas it hath been taken notice that several of the Irish Nation, free men and women, who have no certain place of residence . . . do wander up and down from Plantation to Plantation, as vagabonds, refusing to labour . . . and endeavouring by their example and persuasion to draw servants and slaves unto them of said Nation to the same wicked courses. . ."*
> Daniel Searle, governor of Barbados (1657)

THE IRISH, BOTH servants and slaves, were at the centre of many of the rebellions in Barbados up to the end of the seventeenth century. This is borne out by several statements from governors and the Assembly that some of the Irish were trying to incite their compatriots in the fields to rebellion. The one great fear of all the whites in Barbados, merchants, planters, militia, assemblymen and government officials alike, was that the slaves would revolt and take over the island.

A general uprising took place in Barbados in November 1655. On the sixth of that month, Captain Richard Goodall and Mr John Jones informed the Barbados Council that several Irish servants and slaves, together with some black slaves, had run away from their masters' estates, and were "out in Rebellion in ye thicket and thereabouts". There is no mention of the numbers involved, but they must have been considerable as the Council ordered Lieutenant Colonel Higginbotham "to raise any of the companies of Colonel Henry Hawley's regiment, to follow ye said servants and runaway slaves, and if he shall meet with any of them, to cause them forthwith to be secured, and to send them before the Governor or some Justice of the Peace. But if any of the said servants and runaway Negroes make any opposition, and resist his forces, then to use his utmost endeavours to suppress or destroy them."

It appears from the minutes of the Council that Lieutenant Colonel Higginbotham cannot have been very successful as there are records of runaway servants and slaves launching attacks on the persons and properties of their masters. Planters were ambushed, dragged from their coaches and hacked to pieces with machetes used in cutting the cane. The runaways took the arms of the planters and coachmen and apparently used them to good effect on the militia hunting them down.

The Assembly was particularly concerned about the burning of the sugar fields, the mills and the outhouses, as it struck at the very heart of the economic structure of the island. The number of runaway servants and slaves, both Irish and black, became so great that the governor was asked by the Assembly to mobilise the entire militia. An act was passed on 2 September 1657 to that effect, making it lawful to "kill and destroy such runaways". Several engagements took place; the servants and slaves fought to the bitter end, and often sought death, knowing the tortures that awaited them if taken alive. In one engagement in October of 1657, twenty of the runaways were captured after putting up a fierce resistance, in which twelve militia men and thirty of the runaways were killed. The remainder withdrew into the thickets, carrying their wounded with them. The captives, including six Irishmen, were lodged in the Cage in Bridgetown.

A court was quickly convened, and all the prisoners were condemned to death by fire. On the appointed day, a large crowd gathered to watch the sentence being carried out. Among them were some high-born ladies who were given ringside seats in a special area reserved for members of the Assembly and their guests. The prisoners, stark naked, were nailed to the ground in the form of a cross, with pegs of hardwood driven through their hands and feet. A burning torch was then applied to their feet and moved very slowly up their bodies. They were then beheaded and the heads were displayed on pikes in prominent positions in the market place. The owners were given £25 compensation for each slave killed or executed.

The old minute books of the island show that no more than 20 per cent of the indentured servants who were freed became farmers, overseers or artisans. There is no record of what happened to the remaining 80 per cent: some may have joined the militia, a few became innkeepers or shebeen owners (sellers of illegal liquor) and the remainder were probably the ones described by Governor Daniel Searle as wandering vagabonds, moving constantly from plantation to plantation and inciting their compatriots to rebellion.

Second only to the fear of mutiny was the governor's and Council's fear of the reaction of the Irish in the event of a war with France or Spain. For the Irish, whether free men or runaways, indentured servants or slaves, the best chance of freedom was to escape to the French colonies of the Leeward and Windward Islands. Others joined the pirates in St Lucia, Tobago and Dominica. They stowed away on vessels plying in the region or seized boats at night and cast off. Still others disguised themselves as sailors or soldiers to get aboard military vessels.

In 1675 the Council ordered that an act "be drawn up to prevent the running away of Christian servants and slaves and their getting off by the negligence of such as keep boats or other vessels". The owners of such vessels were required to employ tenants to guard these boats. It became a capital offence for any servant or slave to steal any vessel. Barbadian planters feared that runaway Catholic Irish servants or slaves would not only offer the French critical intelligence concerning the island's fortifications and military strength, but regarded the Irish as treacherous and likely to join with their French and Spanish coreligionists in the event of an invasion. One governor was concerned that the behaviour of these "Bloody Papists", as he put it, would affect the balance of European power in the whole region, especially since several "mulattos, mustees and negroes were, with the Irish, all in league with the French". Daniel Searle issued the following order on September 1652, which confirmed their fears:

> Myself and council having taken into considera-
> tion . . . the considerable number of Irish, freemen
> and Servants, within this Island, and the Dangerous
> consequences, in this Juncture of time, of Wars
> betwixt the Commonwealth of Englande and Spain,
> both in Europe and here. . . that may ensure to this
> Place upon the appearance of an enemy, if the Irish
> and such others as are of the romish Religion, should
> be permitted to have any sort of Arms or
> Ammunition within their Houses or Custody, or at
> any time to wear or go Armed; have thought it nec-
> essary for the better security of this Place, and con-
> tinuance of Peace thereof, to order, that all such as
> are of the Irish Nation . . . be forthwith Disarmed.

In the event of an invasion all the Irish, whether freemen, indentured servants or slaves, were to be rounded up and taken into custody. Church wardens of respective parishes were required "to take account and exact list of all the Irish that live or bee in their Parrishes, and such among them, as are of turbulent, seditious, troublesome, or dangerous spirrits, that they return the names of such to the Governor and Counsell upon Friday next, it being a business of great importancy and consernment to the Peace and security of this Island".

A pass system was introduced and passes were issued to all Irish freemen and women. This carried their particulars, their last occupation and their place of residence. All masters, mistresses and overseers were required to demand that all Irish persons who came to their plantations produce their passes. If they failed to do so, they were to be apprehended, flogged and conveyed to the nearest constable. The pass system did not work, as Governor Searle was informed that runaway Irish servants "that are in rebellion do pass up and down from plantation to plantation with counterfeit and forged testimonials, pretending they are free men or that they have liberties so to pass and, by that means, have opportunity to accomplish their wicked purposes".

Stricter laws were enforced, including branding and the cutting off of the ears of those carrying forged passes. Even this did not stop the runaways, both Irish servants and slaves. In August 1657, Governor Searle complained of the large numbers of Irish still at large and that he was informed by the provost marshal that the Bridgetown Cage was full. Searle demanded still more severe penalties, including execution for runaways. This was granted, and the masters of the runaways were compensated by the public treasurer with rates ranging from £20 to £25 for each executed prisoner.

Because of a constant threat of foreign invasion, each settler was required to have a percentage of white men, English, Welsh or Scots, who could be armed and depended on to fight in such an event. Lord William Willoughby wrote to the Privy Council on 16 December 1667 concerning this matter:

> There yet remaines that I acquainte your Lordships with the greate want of Servants in this Island, if Labour fayle heere. & if the supply be not of good & sure men, the saifety of this place will alwayes be in

question; for though there be noe enemy abroad, the keeping the Slaves in subjection must still be provided for. If your Lordships shall open a trade in Scotland, for transportation of the people of that Nation hither, and prevent any accesse of Irish in the future, it will accomodate all the ends propounded, and abundantly gratify his Majestys good subjects heere.

In other words the Scots were to be used as guards or wardens on the plantations against revolts by Irish and blacks.

The same prejudice against the typical Irish servant or slave of this period is reflected again in the following letter from Lord Willoughby, written in September of the same year: "We have more than a good many Irish amongst us, therefore I am for the downright Scott, who I am certain will fight without a cruxifix about his neck." A letter written in May 1681 from an ordinary planter, Christopher Jeaffreson, sums up the case against the Irish: "Scotchmen and Welchmen we esteem the best servants; and the Irish the worst, many of them being good for nothing but mischief."

In 1686 several Irish slaves were arrested for "being concerned with or privy to an intended rising of negroes to destroy all their masters and mistresses". The objective was to seize Needham Fort, take the arms from it and take over the island. It was a well thought out plot; the slaves chose a number of Irishmen who were to be sent into the fort with money to buy drink for the guards, and having got them drunk, to take the fort by force. All communication with the island was to be then cut off by the sinking of all ships in the harbour to prevent the news of the revolution spreading. Bridgetown was to be burned to the ground and the slaves were to kill all their masters and mistresses. At the last moment the plot was betrayed by a black slave woman who overheard two of the conspirators discussing the details. Apparently this particular slave held a special affection for her mistress. Thirty-six of the leaders, including the Irishmen, were arrested, tortured and then hanged, drawn and quartered. It was the last revolt in which Irish and black slaves took action together.

By the time the census of 1680 was taken, most of the white servants had become freemen and women. Indentured servants were on the way out, and their places were taken by Africans. However, the longed-for freedom did not fill their bellies, and some actually starved to death. The governor of the period, Colonel James Kendall, described their condition in March 1689 in a plea to the Assembly: "They are dominated over and used like dogs, and this in time will undoubtedly drive away all the commonality of the white people and leave the island in a deplorable condition, to be murdered by Negroes or vanquished by the enemy."

He suggested that the freed servants be given two acres of land as was their due (although by the 1680s land was unavailable for them) and the right to a vote, so that members of the Assembly "would sometimes give the poor miserable creatures a little rum and free provisions and such things as would be of nourishment to them and make their lives more comfortable in the hope of getting their vote".

The Assembly contemptuously turned down his request.

CHAPTER ELEVEN

The Cabbage Stalk Soldiers

*"[I]t is not to be denied but the Lord hath greatly humbled us
in that sad loss sustained at Santo Domingo."*
Oliver Cromwell in a letter to Vice-Admiral Goodson (1655)

OLIVER CROMWELL'S "WESTERN Design", which led to the subsequent capture of Jamaica, involved Irishmen, both indentured servants and slaves, firstly as impressed and unwilling soldiers in the expedition against the Spaniards, and secondly as settlers in Jamaica.

Cromwell's grandiose scheme for the capture of all the Spanish-held territories in the West Indies was a flawed one, based almost entirely on inadequate intelligence and unsound advice from men like Martin Noell, Thomas Povey and a man named Thomas Gage. Martin Noell had come a long way from being a poor tobacco planter of 1638. His slaving activities and sugar plantation had made him a very rich man. He left Barbados in 1650 and the following year became an alderman of the City of London and a member of the East India Company. He married John Thurloe's sister-in-law, and this gave him access to the very centre of Cromwellian society. Thurloe, secretary of state and one of the most powerful men in England at the time, was Cromwell's spymaster, setting up an intelligence

131

service that was unequalled in Europe. It is probable that soon after his marriage, Thurloe introduced Noell to Cromwell and he quickly became one of the Protector's favourites. It is evident that Cromwell admired self-made men, as both Noell and Thomas Povey, another Barbadian planter and merchant, were constantly called on for advice on West Indian affairs.

Of the three, Thomas Gage had the most intimate knowledge of the Spanish possessions in both the West Indies and South America. Edmund Ludlow called him "the principal adviser of this undertaking". Gage, who had once been a priest, came from an old English Catholic family; three of his brothers were also priests. He became a Dominican and was sent to Central America as part of the Spanish mission. However, when he returned to England in 1637, he abandoned his religion, became a Protestant and married a wealthy woman. He then wrote a book, *The English–American: a New Survey of the West Indies*, which was published in 1648 and became an immediate best-seller. It dealt with the iniquities of the Spanish Catholics, laity and priests, particularly the Dominicans in Central and South America. He accused the priests of living dissolute lives, drinking, fornicating with native women, burning at the stake such Indians as would not embrace the Catholic faith, and a host of other crimes. This may have been true of Catholic missionary work in the West Indies and South America at the period Gage wrote about, but he also went on to decry Spanish military strength in that continent, stating that nowhere were the Spanish forces in anything like the strength believed in England. Gage stated that his object in publishing the book was to "strengthen the perusers of this small volume against Popish superstition whether in England, or in parts of Europe, Asia or America".

The book brought him to Cromwell's attention, and the Protector was so impressed with it that he had a new edition published in 1653. Cromwell was only too eager to listen to Gage, whose advice suited his own preconceived ideas of the Spaniards' lack of strength in Hispaniola, Cuba, Mexico and South America. Gage's opinion of the Spanish military power, or lack of it, was also echoed by Martin Noell and Thomas Povey. They assured Cromwell that all of the Spanish possessions were plums ripe for the plucking. They told Cromwell that if Hispaniola and Cuba were captured, all the Spanish forces in the whole of Central America could be defeated in less than two years. Only one voice dissented: Colonel John Lambert, an old Ironside who had fought at Marston Moor and in the campaigns in Ireland and Scotland. He warned that the affairs at home and in Ireland should be settled first before embarking on such an expedition of conquest on the other side of the world.

Cromwell was in no mood to listen to cautious advice. "God has brought us where we are," he declared, "to consider the work we may do in the world, as well as at home." He summoned the Spanish ambassador and told him bluntly that England's relationship with Spain could only be assured if the king granted religious liberty to all Englishmen in Spanish territories; he also demanded freedom for English merchants to trade with the Spanish colonies in the West Indies. These demands were completely unacceptable to Spain, as Cromwell well knew they would be, the Spanish ambassador saying that what was being demanded was like asking for the two eyes of the King of Spain. John Milton later wrote of these demands:

> That the motives whereby we have been lately induced to make an attack upon certain islands in the West Indies which have been now for some time in the hands of the Spaniards are exceeding just and reasonable, every one will easily see who considers in hostile manner that king and his subjects have all along, in those parts of America, treated the English nation . . . There are a great many instances of the most cruel and barbarous treatment the English have

133

perpetually met with from the Spaniards in the West Indies, and that even in time of peace.

Milton used very similar sentiments when writing about the Irish nation.

In August 1654 a committee was set up to arrange for the expedition. It was made up of traders like Noell and Povey and sea captains with knowledge of the West Indies. In overall charge was John Desborough, Cromwell's brother-in-law. The Protector, probably lulled by the report of Gage and the others, took little active part in the preparations for what, after all, was going to be his first real overseas expedition of conquest.

The joint commanders of this force were General Robert Venables, who had fought with Cromwell in Ireland, and Admiral William Penn. Penn was only thirty-three when he was appointed, young for an admiral, but he had a good track record, having been Admiral Blake's vice-admiral in 1652 and a hero of the battle of the Downs. In view of the subsequent fate of the expedition, perhaps he will be better remembered as the father of William Penn, the Quaker who founded Pennsylvania.

Thus the expedition, even before it sailed, suffered from one grave defect, a joint command. Traditionally, English sailors do not like soldiers, and Penn was not about to defer to the old soldier, Venables. He must have complained to Cromwell, as the latter wrote to him, "You have your own command full and entire to yourself, nothing interfering with it, nor in the least lessening you." As the expedition was about to sail he wished Penn, "happy gales and prosperous success in the great enterprise you have in hand".

From the beginning General Venables found the greatest difficulty in recruiting men for the expedition. He found that the parliamentary army was loath to release any of its best men, so instead of the old Ironsides he had commanded in Ireland, he was left with the rejects from every regiment. To make up the numbers required he was forced to recruit "vagabonds, rogues, cutpurses and thieves". They were completely untrained and a greater danger to themselves than to the enemy. Mrs Venables, who accompanied her husband, later wrote of them, "the work of God was not to be done by the devil's instruments". To make matters worse, Desborough had not provided enough supplies for the expedition, claiming that supplies would be available in plenty at their first port of call—Barbados.

Three commissioners were appointed to accompany the forces: Edmund Winslow, Daniel Searle and Captain Gregory Butler. Winslow was an experienced man in colonial affairs; now sixty, he had sailed in the *Mayflower* and had been governor of New Plymouth before returning to England. Daniel Searle also had some experience in the colonies, being at the time governor of Barbados. Captain Butler was an unlucky choice: he had been a soldier in Ireland under Essex before emigrating to Barbados. Now in his fifties he was a portly, vainglorious man, and a drunkard. He was described by one of Thurloe's spies named Berkenhead, who accompanied the expedition as scout master, as the "unfittest man for a Commissioner I ever knew employed".

The commissioners were given wide discretion in their choice of attack: Puerto Rico, Hispaniola, Cuba or the Spanish Main. They were told that: "The designe in General is to gain an Interest in that part of the West Indies in the possession of the Spaniard, For the effecting whereof We shall not tye you up to a method by any particular Instructions."

The fleet set sail on 22 December 1654 and arrived in Barbados on 30 January 1655. It was a remarkably fast crossing, particularly for winter. Admiral Penn captured a number of Dutch ships which had not cleared Barbadian waters before its arrival. It was to be the only success of the expedition. General Venables encountered exactly the same problem in recruiting men as he had at home. None of the planters volunteered; they were not about to risk their lives on such an uncertain undertaking. In fact, many actively discouraged it. Berkenhead wrote that "the rich planters, except some few, endeavour all they can to dishearten the men from goeinge . . . some of the planters being of malignant spirits (as indeed most of them are) signifie their follyes in venting their calumnious words against, not only the designe, but the powers by which we come, and the parties employed in it".

Thomas Modyford and Martin Noell either sailed with the expedition or were in Barbados when it anchored, as Berkenhead wrote of the antagonistic attitude of the locals not only to the expedition, but to the two men concerned: "There is in the island, one Colonell Moodiford and Mr Nowell, Secretary of the Island's affairs, who are hugely distasted by this island: for this they two. . . invite our forces over hither, which our islanders are generally against."

Venables also found the greatest difficulty in obtaining arms and provisions for his force. As Berkenhead put it, "[W]e are something disheartened; the islanders either concealing what they have, or being not able to afford a quarter armes for our men; and, we came so badly armed from England." He continues that instead of English pikes, they were forced to accept a great number of half-pikes, "many of them (which may cause your wonder) are made of cabadge stalks; I mean of the trees in Barbados which bear cabages, and this for lack of better wood. They are not all handsome, nor will they long be serviceable, but such as our necessities will admit to furnish ourselves with."

Finally, losing patience, Venables was forced to accept whatever men the island offered. Four companies of the local militia were assigned to go with the expedition, under the command of a Colonel Lewis Morris. As this was not nearly sufficient to make up the numbers required, freemen, indentured servants and white slaves were impressed into service. It was a splendid opportunity for

Daniel Searle to get rid of some of the rebellious Irish, both freemen and indentured servants. For plantation owners, who felt that their malcontent Irish slaves caused so much trouble on any plantation, being "insubordinate, incorrigibly idle and lazy", this was an easy way to get rid of them, especially as the government offered £25 to the planters for every slave and indentured servant thus employed. The Irish were happy to enlist to escape the rigours of life on a plantation. They were armed with the half-pikes made of cabbage stalks and then only when they went aboard ship.

The few planters who did join the expedition were given the ranks of major or captain and the whole motley force was called the "Regiment of Planters". They never drilled together, and Colonel Morris, as Berkenhead puts it, was "not very chearful in the designe", having a young wife "who hath been very importunate with him to leave the voyage".

When at last 3000 men were mobilised, they boarded the ships and the expedition sailed for the Leeward Islands. Here they managed to obtain a few more recruits: 800 from St Kitts, 300 from Nevis and 80 from Montserrat. At St Kitts, Captain Butler, the third commissioner, who had been sent to obtain these recruits, disgraced himself by getting drunk and falling off his horse. "He was so overcome by drink," wrote Venables, "that he fell from his horse and vomitted . . . that the French jeered at His Highness's Commissioners." Here also fights broke out between soldiers and sailors, the soldiers being in a mutinous mood because orders were issued against looting.

Finally the expedition arrived off Hispaniola, where a mixed force of sailors and soldiers, under General Venables, were landed. They found that they were thirty miles from Santo Domingo, their objective, and on the long march the untrained men suffered greatly from heat exhaustion, lack of food and water, and by then most of them were also suffering from dysentery. On the way buccaneers attacked them, or as Venables described them, "a sort of Vagabonds that are saved from the gallowes in Spaine and the king doeth send them heare. These goe by the name of Cowkillers, and indeed it is thayer trad[e]." They managed to beat off the attacks of the Cowkillers, but as they neared Santo Domingo they were attacked by a squadron of Spanish lancers. The Irish and other recruits from Barbados, the "Regiment of Planters", armed with their cabbage stalk pikes, had been placed in the van. When the Spanish attacked with their twelve-foot, steel-tipped lances, the recruits broke and ran, causing panic and disorganisation in the English ranks which followed. The landing party were utterly routed and would have been wiped out but for the brave stand made by the seamen under Vice-Admiral Goodson, who covered their retreat back to their jumping-off point.

A few days later another attempt was made, as futile as the first. Again the Spanish attacked and drove the expeditionary forces back. General Venables was accused of cowardice, and it was reported that he hid behind a tree, "soe much possessed with terror that he could hardlie spake". He certainly was not the man who fought in Ireland and was the victor of Scarifhollis.

Now came the time for recriminations and the apportioning of blame. The commissioners, in a letter to the governor of Barbados, dated 26 April 1655, wrote:

> We are ashamed of the cowardice of our men, and were not the enemy as cowardly as themselves, they might with a few destroy our Army . . . and to say the truth your Men and the men of St Christophers lead all the disorder and confusion . . . Our planters we found most fearful, being only bold to do mischief, not to be commanded as Souldiers, not to be kept in any civil order; being the most prophane debauch'd persons that we ever saw, scorners of Religion, and indeed men kept so loose as not to be kept under discipline, and so cowardly as not to be made to fight.

It is indeed very probable that the rabble from Barbados had no intention of fighting in the first place. The Irish, armed with their cabbage stalk pikes, were no match for the Spanish lancers and almost certainly would have avoided taking part in any engagement, wishing neither to be killed or to kill Spaniards.

Mutual recriminations among the commanders became the order of the day. Venables blamed Penn for faulty seamanship in setting the troops ashore so far from Santo Domingo. Penn accused Venables and the other commanders of incompetence. Certainly they had placed the Barbadians and the other West Indian troops in the van during the advance, and they were always likely to be the first to turn and run. When the disorganised troops retreated to the landing place after the second repulse, General Venables was the first to board, as his wife was in one of the ships. Seeing this, the soldiers refused to allow the seamen to get on board first, as they feared that the fleet, with the general safely aboard, would sail without them. Many died before the survivors of the disaster, and it can only be called that, were safely aboard. It was estimated that more than 1000 men died on that ill-fated expedition, the majority from dehydration, dysentery and fever. The fleet weighed anchor and sailed from Hispaniola on 4 May 1655. There was a great outcry in England when news of the defeat was received there. Cromwell is said to have fallen into such a paroxysm of rage that he dropped down as if dead.

The commissioners, together with General Venables and Admiral Penn, must have felt that they could not return to England without some token of success. They still had 7000 "fighting men" aboard their ships, although their opinion of them was not very high. "They were so cowardly, and not to be trusted or confided in, except rais'd in their Spirits by some smaller success, we did therefore resolve to attempt Jamaica."

Jamaica was an obvious target because it was known to be weakly garrisoned, with a small Spanish population of

2500. The island held no importance in the Spanish conquest of the Americas; it was not a key point in the Spanish defence system, as were Puerto Rico or Cuba. It contained no gold and was used by the Spaniards only as a food supply centre. Its economy was based on cattle rearing, and the salted meat and hides were exported to other Spanish possessions. A small amount of sugar cane was grown, but the sugar was purely for local consumption. A number of Portuguese Jews had settled there in 1580 and become merchants, exporting the hides, tallow and salted meat, and importing olive oil, wine, flour, clothing and hardware.

The first group of Spanish settlers had arrived in Jamaica in 1510, under the captaincy of Diego Columbus, son of the great explorer. They called their chief town Villa de la Vega, which is now known as Spanish Town. When the settlers arrived, there were about 100,000 Arawaks living peacefully on the island, whom the Spaniards attempted to Christianise and enslave. After a few decades, the Arawaks were almost wiped out. Bishop Bartolome de las Casas wrote of the Spanish cruelties in Jamaica, which bore out Thomas Gage's version:

> The islands of St. John and Jamaica, that looked a fruitful garden in 1610 was possessed by the Spaniards with the same bloudy intentions as the others were; for there they also exercised their accustomed cruelties; killing, burning, roasting men, and throwing them to the dogs . . . as if they had come to rid the earth of these innocent and harmless creatures, of whom above 60,000 were murthered in these two islands so lavish were the Spanish swords of the bloud of these poor souls, scarce two hundred more remaining; the rest perished without the least knowledge of God.

The fleet arrived off Jamaica on 10 May 1655 and the troops landed almost unopposed at a place called Passage Fort, the small Spanish force retreating towards Spanish

Town, the capital. Venables and the other army commanders, instead of a swift pursuit, held a council of war. After a couple of wasted days, they advanced warily, always fearful of an ambush. The weak Spanish garrison of less than 1000 men decided to surrender and sent emissaries under a flag of truce to the English commander. Negotiations dragged on for a week, and this gave the inhabitants of Spanish Town time to hide their valuables. It also gave some of the garrison time to retreat into the interior, taking their slaves with them. Under the terms of the surrender, it was agreed that the Spaniards who wished to leave the island were free to do so. The Portuguese Jews chose to remain, and Venables wrote of them, "The Portuguese we hope to make good subjects of; the Spaniards we shall remove." This was against the terms of the capitulation, but the Spaniards were indeed forcibly removed, including the governor, Juan Ramirez. He was an old man in poor health, but despite his pleas to be allowed to remain on the island, he was put aboard ship bound for Campeche and died on the voyage.

When the English soldiers entered Spanish Town, they found few valuables and in revenge destroyed the abbey and all the churches. They then wasted time digging for buried treasure which they never found. Discipline broke down utterly, and the army became a mob. They fanned out from the town, killed more than 20,000 cattle in the countryside and dug up and destroyed the crops planted by the Spaniards. The cattle were left to rot. Their intent was that lack of provisions would force the army command to send them home.

In the meantime Venables became seriously ill, and a council of war decided that he should return to England and personally inform Cromwell of the terrible conditions of the army in Jamaica. Cromwell would not accept any excuses for the failure of the expedition and considered Jamaica almost worthless, a poor return for the expenditure of money and lives that had been lavished on the Western Design. Venables was promptly sent to the Tower, the committal order stating that "General Robert Venables, being General of the English forces sent to America, hath without licence deserted the Army committed to his charge." Admiral Penn, who had returned a few days earlier hoping for an interview with Cromwell to explain his side of the story, was also clapped in the Tower the day Venables was committed, 20 September 1655. Both were kept in solitary confinement for a month, and when Cromwell's rage abated they were released. Neither man was ever given a command again.

Penn retired to his estate in Ireland. Venables recovered his health and, with Mrs Venables busy writing her autobiography, retired from public life. Captain Butler had also returned to England with Venables, and shortly afterwards went back to his estates in Barbados, where he died from the over consumption of alcohol.

Cromwell appointed Major General Robert Sedgewicke in overall command, with Lieutenant General Edward D'Oyley as president of the Council and commander of the army. Sedgewicke was an able and energetic man, but could do little to restore morale to the army. A short time after his arrival he reported to Cromwell: "Our soldiers have destroyed all sorts of provisions and cattle. Nothing but ruin attends them wherever they go. Dig or plant they neither will nor can, but are determined rather to starve than work."

Another correspondent with the expedition wrote to Martin Noell of the conditions prevailing in Jamaica at the time: "Our wants [are] great, our difficulties are many; unruly raw Soldiers, the major part ignorant; lazy dull officers that have a large portion of Pride, but not of Wit, Valour or Authority."

The army would have starved were it not for the fact that a few head of cattle remained. These were slaughtered, along with wild hogs. The Spanish, as was their wont, had brought hogs to the island and had allowed them to run wild as a useful source of food, especially when their supply ships were wrecked or if their food resources dwindled. These were not sufficient, and snakes, lizards and vermin were eaten, together with unripe fruit. This unwholesome diet caused an epidemic of dysentery, and for a considerable time about a hundred men died weekly, Major General Sedgewicke being one of the victims.

Just before he died he wrote to Cromwell that "the state of our Army is sad, as God has visited us with a sore hand of sickness, tearing and snatching us away in much displeasure. . . Unless God in mercy stay his hand it will be very sad with us."

Edmund Winslow, one of the three commissioners, died at sea within sight of Jamaica. Another of those who died was Thomas Gage. He had accompanied the expedition as chaplain, and it is believed that before his death he wished to rejoin the Catholic faith, but no priest could be found since all had been either killed or exiled.

CHAPTER TWELVE

The Irish in Jamaica

"Concerninge the younge women, although we must use force in takeinge them up, yet it beinge so much for their owne goode, and likely to be of soe great advantage to the publique, it is not in the least doubted, that you may have such number of them as you shall thinke fitt . . ."

Henry Cromwell's reply to John Thurloe's request (in accordance with the Protector's instructions) to send 1000 Irish girls to Jamaica (11 September 1655)

JAMAICA WAS NOT, in Cromwell's eyes, the rich prize that had been depicted to him by Penn and Venables on their return to England. None of his grandiose plans for the capture of the rich Spanish possessions in South America or the West Indies had been advanced by its capture. Besides not being a key point in the Spanish Caribbean defence system, neither was it well placed for attacks by the English on the Spanish possessions in the New World.

Sugar cane had been grown from the early Spanish occupation, but very few Spaniards had wanted to settle there, partly because of the climate, but mainly because of the lure of gold in the other Spanish possessions. Consequently, there were only eight sugar mills in operation when the English landed. The Portuguese Jews who had come there in 1580 were the principal traders and continued to be so after the English occupation.

Jamaica was larger than any of the other Caribbean islands previously settled, and the task facing Cromwell and Parliament was how to populate it. A committee was set up consisting of soldiers and merchants to organise the settlement of the island. Cromwell again called on his two advisers on West Indian affairs, Martin Noell and Thomas Povey, which is surprising in view of the poor counsel they had given him regarding the Western Design. They put it to him that the proprietary system (the granting of large tracts of land to those who were prepared to pay for it), under which Barbados and other islands had been planted, was no longer feasible in the case of Jamaica, and that resources of the state would have to be used instead. For a start, all the soldiers with the Western Design expedition, including the "cabbage-stalk" soldiers who were mainly Irish indentured servants and slaves, were to be freed and given thirty acres each. There were, however, not nearly enough of them. Of the 7000 men Venables landed in Jamaica, 3500 had died of various diseases and another 700 had been killed in action against the Spanish and Maroons during the conquest of the island.

In a letter to the commander of the army, Cromwell wrote in November of 1655: "We have sent Commissioners and Instructions into New England, to try what people may be drawn thence. We have done the like to the Windward English Islands; and both in England and Scotland and Ireland, you will have what men and women we can well transport."

Cromwell had as little success with the pioneers in New England as he had when he invited them to settle Ireland a few years previously; only 300 answered his appeal. One of them, named Daniell, was persuaded to write a letter to a friend in New England and describe the island very favourably: "This island farre exceeds all others in America for fertillity in all manner of thingse, fruits and cattle, horses soe good as any in England, and I think farre more plentyfull."

Still the settlers did not come. Cromwell was forced to open the gaols of England and send convicts as slave labour. A consignment of prostitutes collected by the governor of the Tower was shipped with them. They were hardly the best material for settling a new colony. The Standing Committee for Jamaica and the West Indies under the chairmanship of Thomas Povey, with Martin Noell as a leading member of it, then suggested to the Protector that with sufficient inducement, members of the other colonies might be persuaded to come to settle there. Indentured servants were to have their indentures cut short, and select Irish slaves were to be given their freedom if they agreed to go to Jamaica. They were also to be given thirty acres of land. In that way, almost 2000 were shipped to the island to begin work as freemen there.

It is ironic that the very men who profited from the sale of slaves in Barbados, Noell and Povey, were now advocating their freedom. Cromwell, who bore the prime responsibility for sending them there, also advocated their transfer to Jamaica as freemen. He wrote to Governor Searle instructing him to encourage emigration to Jamaica, and as a sweetener declared that Jamaican goods were to be free of customs for seven years in Barbados.

The colonists of Barbados at first did not take kindly to Cromwell's offer. They had been keen to get rid of their rebellious Irish slaves as cabbage stalk soldiers, but now realised that all further shipments of Irish would be directed to Jamaica, leaving them short of labour. Many of the planters solved the problem by moving with their slaves and indentured labour to Jamaica.

John Poyer, in his book *The History of Barbados from the First Discovery of the Island* (1808), wrote: "The conquest of that island, while it opened a wider field for speculation and the exercise of industry, served to drain the population of Barbados in no inconsiderable degree.

Allured by the prospect of greater advantages in a theatre so much more extensive, many opulent planters and other adventurers removed to Jamaica, where land could be procured in greater plenty, cheaper and with less difficulty."

Time-expired servants, both Irish and English, were only too happy to move from Barbados to Jamaica, where they were given thirty acres of land and the tools with which to work it. Colonists from the other settlements in the West Indies contributed their quota. In 1657, Luke Stokes, who had been governor of Nevis, came to the island with a party of 1600 men, women and children who brought their black slaves with them.

The planters from Barbados, Nevis, St Kitts and Antigua immediately went into sugar cane growing and milling. Although Cromwell did not approve of the proprietary system, the size of Jamaica forced him to accept it as the only solution if the island were to be settled. The area of Jamaica is about 3,840,000 acres, but almost two fifths was not fit for cultivation. He was forced to give patents to all whom applied for them, so that by the end of the Cromwellian regime the average size of a plantation was 1000 acres. Even this did not solve the problem—there were still three acres of idle land to every acre under sugar or another crop. Cromwell gave instructions that steps should be taken in Jamaica to avoid the mistakes of a monoculture cultivation and to sow and plant such crops as would produce bread and other food, and thus reduce the heavy expenses of shipping food to the island.

Yet the population was not growing fast enough, and Cromwell again resorted to his old policy of transportation. He ordered his secretary of state, John Thurloe, to find and transport more of the Irish race to Jamaica. The records of the Council of State in England show that they "voted that one thousand girls and as many young men should be lifted out of Ireland, and sent over, to assist in peopling the colony".

Thurloe immediately got in touch with the Protector's

son, Henry Cromwell, then major general of the army in Ireland, requesting him to take steps to meet Cromwell's requirements. Henry Cromwell's reply, still extant among Thurloe's State Papers, is dated 11 September 1655:

> Sir, I received yours of the 4th instant, and give you many thanks for your relation of Jamaica, and though we have mett with some more than ordinary crosse providence in this undertaking, yet I doubt not that but the lord will smile upon it in the issue. I have endeavoured to make what improvement I could in the short time allotted me toucheing the furnishinge you with a recruite of men, and a supply of young Irish girles. In order to it, I have advised with the chief officers near me, not haveinge opportunitie to make it more publique; neither do I think it conveniente, untill I knowe your resolutions more particularly. . . Concerninge the younge women although we must use force in takeinge them up, yet it beinge so much for their owne goode, and likely to be of soe great advantage to the publique, it is not in the least doubted, that you may have such number of them as you shall thinke fitt to make use uppon this account.

On September 18th, he added a postscript:

> I have little to adde to what I writte in my laste . . . I shall not need to repeate anythinge aboute the girles, not doubtinge but to answer your expectations to the full in that; and I think it might bee of like advantage to your affaires their, and ours heer, if you should thinke fitt to sende 1500 or 2000 younge boys of 12 or 14 years of age to the place aforementioned. We could well spare them, and they would be of use to you; and who knows, but it may be a meanes to make them English-men, I meane rather, Christianes.

Here Henry is expressing the Puritan belief of his day that the Catholic Irish were not even Christians. It is also difficult to understand the mentality of these men today, who expected the Irish transported to Barbados and Jamaica to become "English-men", while working as slave labour on their English masters' plantations. Thurloe, acting in the name of the Lord Protector, replied to this letter on 25 September:

> I returne your lordship most humble thanks for the letter I received from you touching transporting of Irish girles to Jamaica; and had thought, that I might by this post have sent the particular encouragements, which my lord protector and the councell will give, for the better enabling your lordship and the councell of Ireland to have proceeded in that business; but I have been prevented therein by my bodily indisposition, and therefore by this can only desire your lordship to proceed as farre as you can, till more particular advices can be sent.

Thurloe's indisposition did not last long and does not seem to have delayed matters much. Early in October, he wrote to Henry Cromwell again:

> I did hope to have given your lordship an account by this poste of the business of causinge younge wenches and youths in Ireland to be sent into the West Indies; but I could not make things readye. The committee of the councell have voted 1000 girles, and as many youthes to be taken up for that purpose; and that there be a summe of money for each head allowed for the clothinge of them, and other necessaryes to the waterside.

The order of council to which Thurloe referred was dated 3 October and stipulated that the "1000 boyes and girles should be shipped at Galway in December, the age fixed in both cases being under 14".

Henry Cromwell replied to Thurloe on 16 October: "I understand by your last letter, that the transportation of a thousand Irish girles and the like number of boyes, is resolved on by councell. . . We shall have (upon the receipt of his highness his pleasure) the number you propownd and more if you think fitt."

Final arrangements were made in November 1655, when Thurloe wrote: "The ships, which are next to goe thither [to the West Indies], will be appointed to take on board them the Irish women or girles. . . The tyme that they must be at port will be about the latter end of December."

What is surprising in all this correspondence is that there is no mention of the Bristol slave traders, on whom Cromwell relied so heavily to transport the Irish to Barbados. When they were in charge of the transportation, the Irish captives were whipped aboard ship half naked, but in this instance a sum of money was set aside for their clothing. Why the change of attitude, and why were "boyes and girles" under fourteen chosen? Was it to make "Christians" of them, or was it because they would fetch a high price in the market place? We shall never know.

Some historians question that they were shipped abroad at all, citing the fact that there are no records of their leaving Ireland. Such records no longer exist because all records of shipments of that period were lost when the Dublin Customs House was burned in 1922. Edward Long, a historian and speaker of the Jamaican House of Assembly in 1768, recorded that the Council of State in England "voted that one thousand girls and as many young men should be lifted in Ireland and sent over, to assist in peopling the colony". He seemed to be in no doubt that the cargo arrived.

In 1922, a woman named Mary Gaunt published a book about Jamaica in New York, entitled *Where the Twain Meet*. In it she writes: "To this boiling pot Cromwell sent 1000 Irish men and 1000 Irish women. I can find nothing but the bare notification that they arrived; and it hardly seems to me that 2000 Irish can have helped matters much, whether they be poor convicts or political prisoners."

We do not know if the 2000 were indentured servants or slaves. Certainly, to judge by Henry Cromwell's saying that, "we must use force in taking them up", they did not sign any indentures willingly. It is probable that the unfortunate girls and boys could not even speak English, so that the indenture document would be meaningless to them in any case. This mattered little when they reached Jamaica. The laws regarding bondsmen were as severe, if not more so, than those governing Barbados or America.

In An Act for Regulating Servants there are the following provisions: "All Servants shall have according to their Contract and Indenture, but where there is no Contract or Indenture, Servants under Eighteen Years of Age at their Arrival in this Island shall serve seven years, and above Eighteen Years of Age shall Serve Four Years, and all Convicted Felons for time of their Banishment." The act also laid down other stipulations; any manservant marrying without the master's or mistress's consent was to serve two extra years. (It is difficult to see how any marriage could take place as there were only a few priests on the island at the time, and they were Spanish and in hiding with the Maroons.) There were also the usual clauses about runaways and the striking of a master or overseer, which followed the practice in Barbados.

A runaway, when captured, was soundly flogged and lost an ear. In addition, for each attempt an extra year was added to his indenture. A persistent runaway was hanged on the plantation as a warning to others. For striking a master or overseer or rebellion, the punishment was death by burning. Sir Hans Sloane, who visited Jamaica between 1687 and 1689, described this punishment in his book *A Voyage to the Islands* (1707): "The punishment of crimes of slaves for Rebellion is by burning them. They are nailed to the ground with crooked sticks on every limb and then applying the fire by degrees from the feet, burning them gradually up to the head, whereby their pains are extravagant."

He also witnessed some of the other types of punishment inflicted on the slaves. Some were whipped with a lance-wood switch till it was broken; another was then used, and, if that broke, it was discarded and still another was taken up. This continued until the skin was broken and blood flowed. Salt and pepper or molten wax was then poured over the back of the victim to add to their torment. Sloane also described the punishments of those who ran away. When they were caught they were put in chains with heavy iron rings around their necks. Sometimes they had iron gags tied to their mouths. Sloane did not seem to be unduly upset by these scenes.

The first years after the conquest of Jamaica were an unsettled time. Although Cromwell had ordered his son, Henry, to send 1500 parliamentary soldiers from Ireland to Jamaica, the military strength of the island was far from adequate. Arthur Granville Bradley, a writer, described the situation at the time:

> Jamaica was for some time in a disturbed condition. The Maroons in their mountain fastness were a constant danger. The British military settlers required a firm hand, while the Catholic Irish prisoners, the unfortunate product of his Irish wars, shipped in batches to the West Indies, were not in a mood to exercise the franchise in a manner conducive to the peace and loyalty of a British colony. Indeed, these drafts may be debited to the wrong side of Cromwell's account in the matter of statesmanship... Idlers and vagabonds too, in all parts of England and Scotland went in daily dread of being seized by the local authorities under Cromwell's orders and shipped to Jamaica, where for the most part, as white slaves, they had to perform work that only Negroes in that climate can accomplish with impunity. Criminals from the gaols, as well as political offenders of all kinds, were shipped out to join the motley throng, among whom the death rate was, of course,

prodigious. A great deal of outrage and cruelty, far
beyond what Cromwell intended, was perpetrated by
individuals exploiting the emigration movement
under loose authority at the expense of objects of
their personal dislike and vengence.

Other Irish people had settled in Port Royal, becoming
innkeepers, butchers, bakers, farriers, metal workers,
builders and a host of other trades people. Some joined the
pirates and rose to become pirate captains in their own
right. It is estimated that 5 per cent of the pirates operating in the Caribbean towards the end of the seventeenth
century were Irish.

After the Restoration things improved in Jamaica, so
that by 1672 there were seventy sugar mills in Jamaica,
producing 700 tons of sugar per year. The planters found
that the black slaves they had brought with them did not
acclimatise as well as they had in Barbados, and it required
an annual turnover of 6 per cent to replenish the work
force. Of course, many of the slaves brought from
Barbados may have been Irish, and that could have
accounted for the high death rate, as it was found that
whites died off much quicker in Jamaica than they did in
Barbados. We do not know how the 2000 Irish boys and
girls shipped from Galway fared, but as the boys were
under fourteen they probably joined the second gang in the
fields, weeding and spreading manure on the crops, or if
lucky, would end up as house boys. And as Prendergast
wrote, the girls were "to be bound by other ties to the soldiers in Jamaica".

The treatment of indentured servants on the island differed little from that of Barbados. An early correspondent
from Jamaica, Charles Leslie, gives this account of their
plight once the ship had anchored: "As we had a great
many Servants on board, and some of them fine
Tradesmen, we had soon a number of the Planters who
came to purchase Indentures. It was affecting to see the
Shoal of Buyers, and how the poor Fellows were made to

pass in Review before their future Tyrants, who looked at them and examined them, as if they had been so many Horses. Each chose whom he liked best; a good Tradesman went off at about £40 and other at £20 per head." Leslie goes on to describe their apparel: "the Servants wear a coarse Osnabrug Frock, which buttons at the Neck and Hands, long Trowsers of the same, a speckled Shirt, and no Stockings."

The drink of "Servants, and the inferior kind of People" was rum punch, "not improperly called Kill-Devil, for Thousands lose their lives by its means". A reference was made to a very similar drink in Barbados in the middle of the seventeenth century, under its old name of "rumbullion". "The chief fudling they make in the Iland is Rumbullion, alias Kill Divill, and this is made of Suggar canes distilled, a hott hellish and terrible liquor." Many of the white overseers and small planters drank this "Kill-Divill" rum, and as a result committed terrible atrocities on their slaves and indentured servants when under its influence. A contemporary gives accounts of some of the sadistic practices:

> Several cruel persons, to gratify their own humours, against the laws of God and humanity, frequently kill, destroy, or dismember their own and other persons' slaves, and have hitherto gone unpunished, because it is inconsistent with the constitution and government of this island, and would be too great a countenance and encouragement to slaves to resist white persons, to set slaves so far upon an equality with the free inhabitants, as to try those that kill them for their lives; nor is it known or practised in any of the Caribbee islands, that any free person killing a slave is triable for his life.

As in Barbados, the hours of work were long, and under the hot sun many of the slaves collapsed and died where they worked in the fields. They were buried where they lay and the work continued. Very often the overseer did not even bother to mention the death of a slave to the owner of the plantation.

The housing, food and the conditions of service varied from estate to estate, depending on the character of the master or overseer. The slave huts were very similar to those built in Barbados, being nine or ten feet long and about six feet wide, and roofed with reeds. The bed was simply a plank which was also used as a table. Sometimes slaves were allowed to make beds constructed from the branches of trees, resting on four posts. The domestic utensils consisted of some calabashes of different sizes for keeping food. In some cases the slaves were allowed to grow their own food, being given a small plot of land beside their huts. They were generally allowed to work on their own plots of land on Saturdays and planted peas, sweet potatoes, cassava, yams and pumpkins. Very often the overseer demanded a portion of whatever they had grown for his own use. He was usually a mulatto or, in some cases, a freed white servant who could find no other employment.

As with Barbados, the Big House of the planter was the focal point of the plantation. However, unlike the former, the slave quarters in Jamaica were within the fortifications which were erected around it. These fortifications were built of sharpened stakes six feet high and surrounded the Big House and all the outbuildings, including the slave huts. They served a dual purpose: to prevent attacks by the Maroons and to prevent the slaves running away and joining up with them. The white free servants were armed and formed a kind of militia within the plantation for the protection of the house and its occupants. Plantations in Jamaica, being spaced so far apart, had no warning signals of an uprising such as existed in Barbados, where the firing of a musket brought help, and consequently each had to rely on its own resources.

An early visitor to Jamaica, a Dr Trapham, described an estate thus:

The stranger is apt to ask what village is it?—for every completed sugar works is no less, the various and many buildings bespeaking as much at first sight; for besides the large mansion house, with its offices, the works, such as the well-contrived mill, the spacious boiling house, the large receptive curing houses, still house, commodious stables for grinding cattle, lodging for the overseer, the white servants, working shops for the necessary smiths, others for framing carpenters and coopers; to all of which, when we add the streets of Negro houses, no one will question to call such complicated sugar works a small town or village.

After the departure of Major General D'Oyley, Lord Windsor was appointed governor in August 1662, and on his arrival published a royal proclamation authorising the grant of thirty acres of land to every free male and female of twelve years of age and over then residing on the island.

Lord Windsor left the island after his short stay because of ill health. On the departure of Windsor, Sir Charles Lyttleton, chancellor of the island, was appointed lieutenant governor, only to be succeeded within months by Colonel Lynch, an Irishman, as president of the Council. Lynch was a far-sighted, astute politician, who endeavoured to foster trade with the Spaniards. He even returned the governor and bishop of Santa Marta, a Spanish colonial city on the north coast of Columbia, who had been brought to Jamaica by some pirates who had sacked the town, to their homes. His was an entire reversal of Cromwell's policy of attacking Spanish possessions. He stated openly that "it was in the English interest that the Spaniards be preserved in their possession of what they have in the West Indies, for their colonies are large and thin of people, so that they cannot take from the English anything they hold". He was well aware that the French were the real danger to the English possessions.

Lynch also called the first meeting of the Assembly. Instead of being open to all freeborn people, its thirty-five members were, like those of Barbados, members of the elite planter and merchant group. They were the white, and wealthy, sugar "plantocracy", and they controlled the Assembly. No freeborn coloured person, no matter how wealthy, could expect to be elected, and, of course, the indentured servants and slaves had no say in the matter, although the Assembly held the power of life and death over them. They passed laws which suited their own interests, and on many occasions came into conflict with the governor. In all the colonies, governors came and went with alarming rapidity. Some died at their posts; others, like young Lord Windsor, left after only a few months because of ill health.

In 1664, Colonel Modyford was appointed governor of Jamaica and was knighted by the king. He was one of the great survivors of his age, having been first of all a royalist officer in England, going to Barbados, and then betraying his royalist principles and Lord Willoughby by forcing the latter to surrender the island to the parliamentary fleet. He remained a fervent parliamentarian and before the Restoration became governor of Barbados, taking over from Daniel Searle. When King Charles II was restored to the throne, Modyford again changed sides and reverted back to being a fervent royalist. Through his cousin, General Monck, who had been created Duke of Albermarle, he received a full pardon for his betrayal in Barbados in 1652. He brought with him from Barbados 800 planters with their slaves and obtained grants of land for them all.

Modyford became an autocratic governor and clashed on several occasions with the elected Assembly. He then dissolved the Assembly and created another of his own choosing. This, in turn, was dissolved because it refused to pass laws inimical to the welfare of Jamaica, and Modyford ruled the island as a despot.

The traffic in Irish slaves continued during the entire reign of Charles II. It was not nearly as great as in the regime of his predecessor, but Irish Tories convicted by the courts were still "barbadoed". None ever returned to their native land and are today all but forgotten by their fellow countrymen.

Cromwell's death and the restoration of Charles II saw a change in the attitude of the governor and the Assembly towards the Catholic Irish in Jamaica. Most of the bond-servants and Irish slaves were freed and given plots of land. Sir Thomas Modyford, then governor, reported to Lord Arlington that a survey of the various parishes in the island showed that 10 per cent of the 717 property holders listed were Irish.

CHAPTER THIRTEEN

The Irish in America

"[I] never saw an Instance of Cruelty in Ten or Twelve years experience in that branch [the African Slave trade] equal to the cruelty exercised upon these poor Irish."
Henry Laureus, planter

CROMWELL, FOR ALL his sins against the Irish, cannot be blamed for transporting the first Irish to America. This dubious honour belongs to James I and his government in Ireland. They carried out with zeal James' injunction: "Root out the Papists and fill it [Ireland] with Protestants."

The first victims of this policy, recorded in the State Papers (Ireland) were 200 Irish political prisoners transported to Virginia in 1620. These were not common criminals but Irish or Anglo-Irish landowners who had been dispossessed of their lands by Sir Arthur Chichester's plantation of Wexford. (Sir Arthur Chichester had already seized the lands of Catholics in Ulster, on the order of King James I.) They had marched to Dublin to protest and for their pains were clapped in gaol by the lord deputy of Ireland to await transportation. In a letter to King James' "most honourable privy Counsaile in England", the lord deputy states in part: "Your Lordships will thereby perceive howe false and malicious their complaints have been, & the good reason wee have to inflict punishment, by committing them to prison. . . [and] in restraining some of them with purpose to send them into Virginia." There is no record of how the Anglo-Irish landlords fared on their arrival in Virginia. It is possible they were sold as indentured servants for a set period of time. If treated as convicts, they would have become liable to servitude for life.

Three years later, in 1623, an anonymous pamphlet called "Advertisements for Ireland", probably written by Sir Arthur Bougchier, also advocated that some of the Irish be sent to Virginia, simply because of the rapid increase in the population: "Though they have not sixpence to live on, they disdain to follow any trade. . . And therefore it may well be feared that so great a multitude of beggars do not break forth to some sudden mischief (which the Lord defend) . . . and if Virginia or some other of the newly discovered lands in the west were filled with them, it could not but serve and raise the country much."

The records in the State Papers (Ireland) show that there was a continuous shipment of Irishmen and women to America during the reigns of James I and Charles I. American and Dutch shipowners carried out a very lucrative trade in indentured servants. One of the earliest planters in Virginia was Danyell Gookin, an Irish landlord from Carrigaline. John Smith, in his *Generall Historie of New England, Virginia and the Summer Isles,* records his arrival: "The 22nd of November [1621] arrived Master Gookin out of Ireland, with fifty men of his own, and thirty Passengers, exceedingly well furnished with all sorts of provisions and cattle, and planted himself at Newport-newes." Gookin had undertaken to transport "great multitudes of people and cattle from Ireland to Virginia".

Danyell Gookin, before emigrating to America, was lord of the manor of Carrigaline, County Cork, where he held extensive estates, and was thus in an excellent position to recruit indentured labour for the colonies. He had his own ships to transport both indentured servants and cattle and did not have to rely on American or Dutch transports. After fighting in the Indian wars, Gookin returned to Ireland, but retained his plantation in Virginia, which passed on to his son.

When his son Daniel took over the plantation in 1630, he continued with the importation of cattle and indentured servants. Daniel the Younger, as he was called, later rose to prominence in the political and military affairs of Massachusetts Bay Colony. (It is interesting to note that descendants of Danyell Gookin still live in Salem, Oregon, and that Richard Gookin, a historian, has written a *History of the Gookin Family*, published in Salem in 1991.)

The indentured servants who sailed in the Gookin ships were lucky, as Danyell and his son treated them well, with ample food and accommodation during the eight to ten weeks voyage. Not so lucky were other indentured servants who were transported from Ireland in American or Dutch ships, the so called "hell-ships".

The American historian, Lerone Bennett Jr, in his book *The Shaping of Black America* (1974), gives a graphic account of immigrant ships: "They came, these Christian demi-slaves, the same way most blacks came, crammed shoulder to shoulder, toe to toe, the living and the dead side by side, in the unventilated holds of crowded ships. In this respect, as in others, there were striking similarities between the white servant trade and the black slave trade. (It was not for nothing that the trade in Irish servants was called the Irish Slave trade.)"

Sometimes more than half of the servants died before the ships reached America. When the ships finally docked, the survivors were lined up on deck for inspection by prospective buyers. An American writer, Abbott Emerson Smith (1947), described the scene that followed: "The servants were produced from their quarters and the prospective purchasers walked them up and down, felt their muscles, judged their states of health and morality, conversed with them to discover their degree of intelligence and docility, and finally, if satisfied, bought them and carried them home...The whole scene bore resemblance to a cattle market."

The indentures of these Irish men and women were bought by American tobacco planters. As they did not speak English, the Irish had no idea of what they were signing and very often marked with a cross an indenture that bound them to servitude for ten to twenty years, all legal in the eyes of the law.

Once the sale had been completed, the Irish indentured servants were owned, body and soul, by the planter who bought them. They were slaves to the end of their indentures. An American writer, T.J. Wertenbaker, in his book *Patrician and Plebeian in Virginia* (1910), wrote that "the indentured servants... were practically slaves, being bound to the soil and forced to obey implicitly those whom they served".

Another American writer quoted by Bennett, J.B. McMaster, goes even further. "They became in the eyes of the law a slave and in both the civil and the criminal codes, were classed with the Negro and the Indian. They were worked hard, were dressed in the cast off clothes of their owners, and might be flogged as often as the master and mistress thought necessary."

Certainly this was the opinion of most of the white planters, who ordered their overseers to work them hard and treat them as they treated their black slaves. In fact they were treated worse than the black slaves. A contemporary writer, William Eddis, in a letter written in 1770, said: "Negroes being a property for life, the death of slaves in the prime of youth and strength is a material loss to the proprietor. . . They are therefore under more comfortable circumstances than the miserable Europeans over whom the rigid planters exercise an inflexible severity. . . Generally speaking, they [the white servants] groan beneath a worse than Egyptian bondage."

There were few penalties for cruelties to indentured servants. One planter was taken to court for hanging a servant up by the heels as butchers do beasts for the slaughter. The penalty? He was "rebuked" by the court. Another planter, charged with beating his servant to death, was acquitted by the court because there had been provocation on the servant's part. Masters were allowed to flog both female and male servants "until the blood flowed". In a case of disobedience they were permitted to severely whip the offender and then nail him by the ears to a pillory.

Runaway servants were treated with extreme harshness. A law in Maryland passed in 1639 stated that a servant convicted of running away was to be publicly executed. A law passed in Virginia in 1642 declared that a servant who ran away for the second time was to be soundly flogged and branded on the cheeks or shoulder with the letter "R".

Despite the penalties, servants still ran away. They left the plantations late at night, stealing food and clothing to help them on their way. They travelled at night, hiding out in bush or forest during the day and swimming rivers to throw off the pursuit of hunters with dogs. Some fought to the death, preferring it to the floggings and other barbarities that would ensue if they were captured. The papers of the colonial period are full of advertisements for runaway indentured servants. Here is just one of them:

> Ran Away, from the subscriber, living on Monocacy, Carroll's Manor, in Fredrick County, 6 miles from Fredrick town on the 27th December last, an indented Irish Servant Man, known by the name of Patrick Quigley, a shoemaker by trade, of middling stature, well set, of ruddy complexion, short black hair, about 5 feet 2 or 3 inches high, 24 years of age; had on and took with him when he absented a felt hat half worn, short blue sailor's jacket, red waistcoat, pair of white cloath breeches, a pair of white and a pair of black speckled milled stockings, and a pair of old shoes with steel buckles. Whoever takes up the Said Servant

and brings him to the subscriber or secures him in any goal, so that his master may get him again shall have, if taken 20 miles from home, Twenty shillings, if thirty miles Thirty shillings, and if a farther distance Three Pounds, including what the law allows, and reasonable charges if brought home to Daniel Hardman, January 8, 1785.

One wonders if Patrick Quigley was ever caught and, if so, what punishment he endured. Certainly, Mr Hardman was willing to expend a lot of money to get him back. There was no difference between the advertisements for runaway indentured servants and slaves.

As in Barbados, the conditions under which they lived varied from plantation to plantation, but, as Lerone Bennett Jr points out, it was generally harsh. It must be remembered that race and religion played an important part in their treatment. The plantation owners were men of the English upper class seeking to make their fortune in America and were, to a man, Protestant. They regarded the Irish as savages and their religion as unchristian and riddled with superstition. Bennett notes that the first white settlers were organised around concepts of class, religion and nationality.

> To come right out with it America—in the beginning—was a land of the hunted and the unfree. For almost two hundred years the land was inhabited largely by a population of black, red and white bondsmen. Most of these bondsmen, in the beginning, were indentured servants. That is to say, they were temporary slaves who sold themselves, or were sold by others, to the colonies or individual planters for a stipulated number of years (five, seven or more) in order to pay the cost of their passage.

The indentured servants lived in log huts, nine or ten feet long by six feet wide, roofed over with reeds, the door being the only opening. The beds were made of branches of trees, interwoven and resting on four posts. The domestic utensils consisted of calabashes of varying sizes to keep food. For breakfast they received a hunk of coarse bread. The midday meal was a bit of cold bacon or rotting fish, and they usually ended up with boiled Indian corn at nighttime—the dreaded loblolly. They were worked to excess, summoned from their sleep at first light, marched to the tobacco fields and forced to work until dark. They were given a half hour at midday to swallow their cold bacon or fish, and when darkness fell they were marched back to their huts, there to light fires to boil their Indian corn.

In the early days of Virginia, and later of Maryland and New England, the elite planters made no distinction between white indentured servants and black slaves. As Lerone Bennett Jr describes it, white masters held the black and white labouring classes in equal contempt and exacted the same work from both groups.

Like Barbados, the whip, the symbol of the master's authority, was in daily use, wielded by blacks, mulattos or poor whites who had completed their indentures. Bennett writes that it was not unusual in those days for a white master to force a white woman to marry a black male servant. Nor was it unusual for a white master to give a black man a position of authority over white male and female servants. They often exceeded their authority, and it was not unusual for a black driver to flog a white man until he became unconscious, for some small fault or imagined slight.

Philip A. Bruce, in his *The Economic History of Virginia in the Seventeenth Century* (1896), wrote that: "the life which slaves followed as agricultural labourers could not have differed essentially from that of the white servants engaged in the performance of the same duties; the task expected of both were the same, and in the fields, at least, no discrimination seems to have been made in favour of the latter".

In the early days of the plantations, blacks and whites lived side by side with the resulting sexual intimacy.

Consequently, according to a contemporary writer, Peter Fontaine, "Colonial Virginia swarmed with mulatto children." Of course, the white planters exploited the black women servants, but there is also evidence that male white indentured servants either mated with or married black women.

James Hugo Johnson, in his study, *Race Relations in Virginia and Miscegenation in the South*, wrote:

> [T]he association of the indentured servant and the slave was very close. They were often subjected to the same treatment and held by the master in the same esteem. Such associations led to many of the marriages that have been recorded. In those colonies where the numbers of the Negro slaves were comparatively few and when the master's only interest in his indentured servant was in the profits of his labour, many masters must have been little concerned to prevent the inter-mixture of the two races. Many instances of this lack of interest in race relations could, no doubt be discovered throughout the entire Colonial period.

An observer in the beginning of the eighteenth century wrote: "Many respectable citizens, who are reduced in temporalities; on their decease their poor orphans are bound out in gentlemen's homes, where the maid servants are generally white, the men servants are black, and the employers allow the blacks as many liberties as they think proper to take; and no distinction is made between the white girls and black men."

It would appear that some white planters actively promoted miscegenation, so that the children of such unions would later become workers on their plantations. James Hugo Johnson claimed that the larger part of such race mixture was due to the union of black males and white females.

Philip A. Bruce maintained: "The class of white women who were required to work in the fields belonged to the lowest rank in point of character; not having been born in Virginia and not having thus acquired from birth a repugnance to association with Africans upon a footing of social equality, they yielded to the temptations of the situations in which they were placed."

Bruce, in another statement, said: "The system of indentured service in its social effects differed but little, if at all, from the system of slavery. It really accentuated the social divisions among the whites more distinctly than the presence of the institution of slavery did. . . It gave purely class distinctions a recognised standing in the colonial courts of law."

The gulf between the masters and their white servants grew larger as the century progressed. Lerone Bennett put this very well: "Not only were white servants the basis of the wealth of the early colonies; they were also the basis of a huge and growing system of servility. By the last decade of the seventeenth century, servitude had become part of the fabric of America, and the famous settler syndrome—arrogance, protofascism, insensitivity to human needs, and a tendency towards unreality—was well developed."

The poor white syndrome continued through the eighteenth and into the nineteenth century. Indentured servants were considered, first and foremost, as the wealth of the planter. His standing in the community was judged by the number of indentured servants he owned. Governor Horatio Sharpe of Maryland said in 1756 that "the planters' fortunes here consist in the number of their Servants, (who are purchased at high Rates) much as the Estates of an English Farmer do in the multitude of Cattle".

It was only when the indentured servant system was dying out that the wealth of a planter was judged by the number of black slaves he held. At the end of the eighteenth century the flood of Africans had reached its peak. Just before the Revolution, the black slaves numbered 40 per cent of the population of Virginia, 60 per cent of the population of South Carolina, and 30 per cent of the population of Maryland. The first census ever taken in America, in 1790, showed that there were 737,000 African slaves in America, almost 20 per cent of the total population of 3.9 million people. The days of the Irish indentured servants in America were over.

CHAPTER FOURTEEN

The Irish Buccaneers

"The place was a gilded hades, and mammon held sovereign sway over its people. Bearded seamen, bronzed and weather-stained, bedecked with priceless jewellery and the finest silks of the Orient, swaggered along its quays and gambled with the heavy gold coins whose value no one cared to estimate . . . Common seamen hung their ears with heavy gold rings studded with the costliest gems . . . And every man in that crowd of pirates lived beneath the shadow of the gallows."
A contemporary account of Port Royal by a traveller named Henderson in the latter half of the seventeenth century

THE NAME BUCCANEER came from the word *boucan*. The Caribs and Arawaks of the West Indies cured their meat by drying it in the sun. They then laid it in long strips on a wooden grate and smoked it over a slow fire of green wood, the cured meat being called *boucan*. It was thought that the Caribs, a fierce and bloodthirsty race, before the arrival of the Spanish and later the Dutch and English, first perfected this method by killing their enemies and then boucanning their bodies for later consumption. Père Labat referred to this practice in his description of his travels through the West Indies in the seventeenth century. They told him that Frenchmen made the most delicate eating while Spaniards were the most difficult to digest. There

171

is no mention of Englishmen, although as late as the time of Labat's travels, the Caribs were raiding English settlements and carrying off prisoners to be boucanned. Their own word for boucanning was *barbacoa*, from which we get the word barbecue.

Perhaps it is interesting to note here that Labat was not the naive missionary he pretended to be. This Dominican priest, when visiting Barbados, stole a plan of the island and made detailed notes of its fortifications and military strength. He considered that the French could capture Barbados with 5000 Creoles (West Indian-born Frenchmen), together with the help of about 1000 buccaneers. In such an event, the Irish in the colony would have risen to a man to join them.

The original buccaneers began as hunters of wild cattle, and they were the "Cowkillers" who attacked Venables' forces on their way to Santo Domingo. Venables' claim that they were all Spanish was erroneous; there were many Frenchmen among them. They made a living for a time by slaughtering cattle, boucanning the meat, and selling it to passing ships. The Spaniards in Santo Domingo tried and failed to wipe them out, but the buccaneers were excellent shots and inflicted heavy losses on them. They did, eventually, get rid of them by killing the cattle from which the buccaneers made their living. This engendered a hatred of the Spanish, which would cost them dearly in the end.

The buccaneers were now forced to take to the sea. At first using rowing boats and creeping up on small Spanish coastal vessels, using surprise as their main tactic, they attacked and killed the crews and took the ships. They were utterly ruthless and cared nothing for their own lives or the lives of their victims. Using the small coastal vessels, they attacked larger ships, again at night with the element of surprise. In this way they were eventually able to acquire vessels of thirty or forty guns.

Driven out of Hispaniola (now Haiti), the buccaneers established their headquarters on the island of Tortuga, off the north-west coast of Hispaniola. From there, they wreaked such havoc among Spanish shipping that the latter sent a strong force from Santo Domingo against them. They took the island and massacred the 600 white men, women and children living there. However, they did not leave a garrison on the island, and the buccaneers who were at sea returned and again occupied it, becoming in time more numerous than before. They were a mixture of Frenchmen and Englishmen, with the French predominating. The French, anticipating another attack by the Spaniards, appealed to the French governor of St Kitts, de Poincy, for help. Chevalier Lonvilliers de Poincy had been appointed by the King of France as his lieutenant general for all the "American Islands" and captain general of St Kitts. He was only too happy to accede to the Tortugan's request, as he happened to have on his staff a Huguenot by the name of Monsieur le Vasseur, whose religion was objected to by both the French government and many of the French settlers in St Kitts. The ideal solution was to send him as governor to Tortuga. He proved to be an able man who, from 1640, ruled the lawless community for twelve years, building up the fortifications of the island.

The most detailed record in existence of the buccaneers in Tortuga, Hispaniola, and later Jamaica was one written by a man named A.O. Exquemelin, a Dutchman, who was himself a buccaneer although, as he explains in *The Buccaneers of America*, for want of anything better. Exquemelin had been an indentured servant with the French West India Company, which had taken possession of Tortuga in 1664. It had traded on credit but could not gain payment and therefore was forced to close and sell all its goods, even its indentured servants for twenty or thirty pieces of eight. One of these was Exquemelin, whose book describes how many turned to piracy.

As a servant of the Company myself, I was among those sold, and had just the ill luck to fall into the hands of the wickedest rogue in the whole island. He was the deputy governor or lieutenant-general, and he did me all the harm he could think of. He even made me suffer intense hunger, depriving me of my food. He wanted me to buy my freedom for 300 pieces of eight, offering to let me go for that amount.

Finally, I fell into a severe illness through all the discomfort I'd been through, and my master, fearing I should die, sold me to a surgeon for seventy pieces of eight. When I began to recover my health, I had nothing to wear except an old shirt and a pair of drawers. My new master was considerably better than the first. He gave me clothes and everything I needed, and when I had served him a year he offered to set me free for 150 pieces of eight, agreeing to wait for payment until I had earned the money.

When I was free once more, I was like Adam when he was first created. I had nothing at all, and therefore resolved to join the privateers or buccaneers, with whom I stayed until the year 1670, accompanying them on their various voyages and taking part in many important raids.

Exquemelin's book, first published in Amsterdam in 1678, was a great success and translations followed in German, Spanish, French and in English, this last version appearing under the anglicised version of his name, John Esquemeling.

His is a vivid a contemporary account of what a buccaneer's life was like in the latter half of the seventeenth century, providing a description of the origins, lives and exploits of the buccaneers. There has been considerable discussion about its veracity, but in his introduction to the 1925 edition, Andrew Lang wrote that "where Exquemelin's facts may be checked from State Papers or independent witnesses they tally". Peter Earle in his *The Sack of Panama* (1981) wrote that "Exquemelin gets all the Spanish names right for the forts in Santa Catalina and . . . his general account is very accurate. He gets nearly all the dates wrong, which is forgivable considering he must have written his account some time after the event. He is also guilty of some very tall stories which are normally quite easy to detect."

Sir Alan Burns, in his *History of the British West Indies* (1954), wrote of the buccaneers: "The most important influence on West Indian history was the dramatic rise to power of the buccaneers, who contributed in no small degree to the protection of the English, French and Dutch colonies into their early days, and the weakening of Spanish control in the Caribbean. Whatever their crimes, and they were many, for more than half a century they dominated be West Indian scene."

Kipling wrote of them:

> Then said the souls of the gentleman-adventurers –
> Fettered wrist to bar all for red iniquity:
> "Ho, we revel in our chains
> O'er the sorrow that was Spain's!
> Heave or we sink it, leave or drink it,
> We are masters of the sea!"

As Burns noted, the buccaneers were certainly no gentlemen. Their hatred of all the Spaniards knew no bounds, and they often showed little mercy to any Spanish ship they captured. Although pirate films show buccaneers forcing prisoners "to walk the plank", a short piece of wood suspended over the ship's side, this was seldom practised; drowning was considered too merciful a death for the Spaniards. The buccaneers preferred the more refined cruelties such as roasting on a gridiron, or "death by a thousand cuts": suspending the naked prisoner in a net suspended from the yardarm, and slashing at him with the sabres until he expired. The women were used as sex slaves by the seamen for the duration of the voyage and when it ended had their throats cut.

It has been written that buccaneers, unlike the pirates who came after them, never attacked ships of their own nationalities. This is nonsensical, as the crews of a buccaneer ship consisted of many nationalities—and their only object in life was plunder. The French writer, Justamond, wrote: "In cases of extreme necessity they attacked the people of every nation, but fell upon the Spanish at all times."

In times of war the buccaneers were granted commissions and turned into privateers to fight for the French or English, reverting when peace came to their old profession of buccaneering. The buccaneers were almost an international organisation, French predominating, but including English, Dutch, Portuguese and Irish. The Irish were composed of runaway indentured servants, some of whom had completed their indentures, and Irishmen who had been sold as slaves in Barbados and who had managed to escape. They became "Brethren of the Coast", as the buccaneers were called, because there was no other life open to them. Many of them were soldiers of the Irish armies who, after the final defeat by the Cromwellian forces in 1652, refused to go abroad and became Tories. For this, when caught, they were transported as slaves. They were accustomed to hard living, and above all, knew how to use the weapons of the period: the cutlass, pistol and musket. Some had been gunners, a valuable asset, and all were welcomed by the buccaneers of Tortuga and later in Port Royal.

Perhaps the most ruthless and bloodthirsty buccaneer that ever sailed out of Tortuga was a Frenchman, François L'Olonnois (or L'Ollonais). He was born at a place called Les Sables d'Olonnais on the French coast and was shipped out to St Christopher, one of the Caribbean Islands, as an indentured servant. Indentured servants in the French possessions were treated no better than those in the English. However, he survived his term of indenture and made his way to Hispaniola where he worked as a "Cowkiller" for some time. Expelled with the other buccaneers, he went to Tortuga where he joined a pirate ship. After a couple of voyages, in which his courage and daring were noted by every member of the crew, he was given a ship of his own.

The Franco-Spanish War was being fought at the time, and L'Olonnois fought and won many battles with Spanish ships. Such was his courage and daring that, although often out-gunned, he and his followers closed in on Spanish ships and took them with cutlass and pistol. His name became a byword for cruelty. At one time, he cut a prisoner open, ripped his still beating heart out, gnawed it and then flung it in the faces of the other prisoners, telling them that the same fate awaited them if he didn't get the information he wanted. He returned to Tortuga an acclaimed hero. As did all the buccaneer captains, he divided the booty fairly among his men and paid them for the loss of a limb or their sight. Then began three weeks of revelry, drinking and whoring before setting out on his next expedition.

It was on this expedition that he picked up a boat carrying four white slaves from Barbados. These Irishmen had somehow managed to steal a boat and put to sea, hoping to sail to Tortuga. They were led by a man named "Red Legs" Greaves, a former soldier in the Catholic Confederation army, who, refusing amnesty to go to Spain with the others, became an outlawed Tory. Not much is known of the background of Greaves. The name is not an Irish one, but he may have been of Anglo-Irish descent. He must have had some education, as he spoke French fluently. The date of his capture and transportation is also uncertain, but the practice of hanging captured Tories was gradually abandoned; they were found to be more valuable as merchandise to be sold to Barbadian planters. Greaves was shipped out with 300 others and sold to a planter with a record for cruelty. He was frequently flogged for insubordination. Finally, he was sold to a merchant and sent to hard labour on the wharves.

He and his three companions must have plotted their escape carefully. Despite Governor Daniel Searle's orders for a strict watch to be kept on all vessels, some were still left poorly guarded. While loading sugar on to ships in Bridgetown, Greaves saw a lugger with only one guard on it. He and the three others slipped their chains by greasing their legs with tallow, killed the watchman and set to sea. They had between them some rations of coarse bread which they had hoarded and a cask of water they found on the lugger. One of Greaves' companions had been a mariner and was able to set sail for Tortuga. They never reached it, as, one hundred miles out, they were intercepted by L'Olonnois' ship. As it drew closer the watch was surprised to be hailed in French by the tall, red-haired man who appeared to be the captain of the lugger. He was invited aboard and, in L'Olonnois' great cabin, told his story. The Frenchman was happy to enrol the men in his crew, and they fought with him for two years. Greaves' bravery and knowledge of battle tactics impressed the Frenchman, who eventually made him captain of a small ship in his flotilla and gave him his master mariner and the two other men who accompanied him as part of his crew.

After another two years, in which they boarded and killed the crews of several Spanish ships, L'Olonnois and his fleet of ten ships and over 600 men, returned to Tortuga. The usual drinking and wenching took place and when it was ended, L'Olonnois decided to split up his flotilla, giving each of his captains command of a ship. On his last expedition he tried to intercept a Spanish gold ship, but was set upon by both the Indians and the Spaniards just on the mouth of the river Nicaragua. L'Olonnois fled, but on arrival in the Gulf of Darien, he and his remaining men fell into the hands of those the Spaniards called *Indios Bravos*. According to one man who somehow managed to get away, L'Olonnois was hacked to pieces and boucanned.

When news of his death reached Tortuga, the captains of his flotilla felt free to "go on the bounty" on their own. Greaves replaced most of his French sailors with Irishmen, escaped slaves, indentured servants and freemen he found in Tortuga. For another two years he ranged the Caribbean, plundering not only Spanish but English ships for which nation he held a special hatred. He landed the crews of the Spanish ships on the nearest land, but sent the English ships, together with their crews, to the bottom of the sea.

However, Greaves grew tired of piracy; he was an outlaw because of his attacks on English ships. He led his men on one last expedition, an attack on the island of Margarita, and plundered the city, sparing the lives of the inhabitants but leaving with a fortune in gold and jewels. He then set sail for the island of Nevis, where he handed over his ship to his master mariner and settled down as a respectable planter.

Patrick Kelman Roach, in his book *The Bridge Barbados* (1976), wrote of Greaves: "One of these white slaves who escaped bore the name of Red Legs Greaves and history has stated that it was he who was responsible for capturing and looting the island of Margarita which lies off the Venezuelan coast and was rich in pearls even at that time. After this he is supposed to have retired with his loot and lived the life of an honourable planter in Nevis."

Another Irish pirate of whom we have some knowledge was a man called Plunkett. In 1650 he was operating off Barbados and even entered Bridgetown harbour, stole a ship and destroyed some of the fortifications, as a result of which the authorities were forced to strengthen the island's coastal defences. Ligon mentions him in his book *A True and Exact History of the Island of Barbados* (1657). He recounts that on his departure from the island on 15 April 1650 at midnight, "which time our master made choyce of that he might better pass undescryed by a well known Pirate, that had for many days layn hovering about the Island, to take any ships that traded with London, by virtue of a commission, as he pretended, from the Marquis of Ormond. This Pirate was an Irish man, his name Plunquet, a man bold enough; but had the Character of being more merciless and cruel then became a valiant man."

Plunkett seems to have made a habit of boarding and sinking English ships and impressing the crew. Those who did not wish to join him went to the bottom with their ships. This commission which Ligon mentions was the type held by many pirates of different countries and gave the bearer an apparently legal right to attack and plunder.

It is indeed possible that Plunkett held a commission from Ormonde, acting on behalf of Charles II. On the other hand, Philip Gosse in his book *The Pirates' Who's Who* (1924), wrote: "Often the commission or letter of marque carried about so jealously by some shady privateer was not worth the paper it was written on, nor the handful of doubloons paid for it."

When the pirates transferred their operations from Tortuga to Port Royal in Jamaica, their presence was tolerated and sometimes even encouraged by the authorities. In more than one instance, we have government ships operating with pirates. A classic example is that of Lord Thomas Windsor who sent two of his ships under Commodore Myngs to join the pirate Whetstone in an attack on the Spanish possession of Santiago de Cuba.

Windsor arrived in Port Royal in August of 1662. The thirty-five year old was the first royalist governor of Jamaica. He immediately began to make changes to the politics of the region. He had been given secret instructions from Charles II himself to the effect that if "the King of Spain shall refuse to admit our subjects to trade with them, you shall in such case endeavour to procure and settle a trade with his subjects in those parts by force". Some days after his arrival Windsor sent letters to the governors of the Spanish settlements demanding that they admit English merchantmen into their ports.

Both Charles II and Windsor already knew that this would be refused. Although peace existed between England and Spain at the time, Windsor made privateering commissions available "for the subduing of all our enemies by sea and by land". He appointed Commodore Myngs as head of a strike force against the Spanish settlements and soon had 1300 men as volunteers. History does not tell us if any of them were Irish, but it is more than likely that many of the smallholders were only too willing to leave their toil in the expectation of booty. Thus, the *Centurion*, the ship that brought Windsor to Jamaica, and another smaller one called the *Griffin* were joined by ten privateers, including another small ship commanded by the twenty-seven-year-old Henry Morgan. There was very little to choose between privateering and outright piracy. Cotton Mather, a Puritan clergyman and writer from Boston, complained that "The Privateering Stroke so easily degenerates into the Piratical, and the Privateering Trade is usually carried on with an UnChristian Temper and proves an Inlet into much Debauchery and Iniquity". A private warship was usually financed by merchants ashore who received so many shares in the vessel's future loot in return for their capital investment. Big plunder, big dividends. No plunder, no dividends. In practice when in operation, they used the technique of surprise and board, preferably without cannonade to avoid damaging what they hoped would be their own future property. Many outright pirates like Henry Morgan and Blackbeard started their careers as privateers.

Myngs' plan of attack against Santiago de Cuba was ably assisted by a Sir Thomas Whetstone. This man was a nephew of Oliver Cromwell but had remained a royalist for the duration of the war. Under the Restoration of Charles II, Whetstone received £100 from the king to settle his gambling debts and was then forced to emigrate to Jamaica, where he immediately turned to piracy.

Myngs and his ships left Port Royal on 1 October 1662 with twenty vessels and on 16 October arrived off Santiago de Cuba. They managed to land 1000 men and, in Myngs' own words:

> At the entrance of the town, The Governor Don Pedro de Morales, with 200 men and two pieces of ordnance stood to receive us, Don Christoper [de

Issasi Arnaldo] the old Governor of (Spanish) Jamaica with 500 more being in reserve. We soon beat them from their station and with the help of Don Christoper, who fairly ran away, we routed the rest. Having mastered the town we took possession of the (seven) vessels in the harbour, and the next day I dispatched parties in pursuit of the enemy and sent orders to the fleet to attack the harbour, which was successfully done, the enemy deserting the great castle after firing but two muskets.

The privateers, on finding little booty, levelled the castle to the ground as a reprisal and sailed back to Port Royal triumphantly. Windsor had little time to greet them as he was already on board a ship bound for England. His tenure as governor had lasted three months.

After Windsor's departure Colonel Thomas Lynch, who was president of the Council in Jamaica, became acting governor, but in 1664 Colonel Modyford was made a baronet and appointed governor of Jamaica. The old turncoat was forgiven and because of his experience of sugar planting and manufacture in Barbados was able to introduce the industry into Jamaica. The king wrote to him on his appointment in June 1664 condemning the buccaneers who had by then transferred their headquarters from Tortuga to Port Royal. His view was that he could not "sufficiently express his dissatisfaction at the daily complaints of violence and depredations done by ships, said to belong to Jamaica, upon the King of Spain's subjects" and Modyford was "strictly commanded, not only to forbid the prosecution of such violencies for the future, but to inflict condign punishment on offenders, and to have entire restitution and satisfaction made to the sufferers".

Modyford issued a proclamation in the sense of the king's order, but it was largely ignored. It was even rumoured that the king became a partner in the buccaneering expeditions and shared in the loot.

Henry Morgan, a Welsh indentured servant in Barbados

(although Morgan in later life denied this), joined the buccaneers in Tortuga on the completion of his indentures, and because of his reckless bravery and cunning, quickly rose in their ranks until he eventually became vice-admiral. He led the raids on Puerto Bello in 1668, where he forced nuns and priests to carry ladders which were placed against the walls of the strongly defended forts. The Spaniards hesitated to fire until the ladders were in place, and Morgan and his men scaled them and slaughtered the defenders. In the following year he sacked Maracaibo. In 1671 he sacked and burned Panama, torturing and slaughtering the defenders. However, the raid on Panama took place three days after the signing of the Treaty of Madrid, and when Morgan arrived in Jamaica he found that Governor Modyford had been arrested and sent to England to the Tower, where he languished for two years. Governor Sir Thomas Lynch, an Irishman, who did his best to foster relations with the Spaniards, replaced him. Morgan was later arrested and sent to England, but was freed on his arrival there, owing to popular sentiment on his behalf and Morgan's defence that he had not know about the treaty. So great was that sentiment that Morgan was knighted and returned to Jamaica in 1674 as lieutenant governor of the colony, with instructions to root out piracy.

Exquemelin's contemporary account of Morgan's adventures does him no favours. Peter Earle notes:

> The main general problem with his account is his assessment of Morgan. He goes out of his way to blacken the Admiral's name and to give him a reputation which is not sustained even by the Spanish evidence. The motive for this is quite clear. Exquemelin, like many of the privateers, thought that he had been cheated by Morgan after Panama, and the book is a very good way of getting his own back. The English publishers of Exquemelin were forced to retract most of the defamatory material after a libel suit was settled out of court in 1685 and it seems probable that

they were only doing Morgan justice in doing so. But subsequent editions have repeated Exquemelin's libels, and Morgan's name has suffered to this day as a result.

Sir Hans Sloane described him in 1688 as "lean, sallow-coloured, his eyes a little yellowish, and Belly a little prominent, much given to drinking and sitting up late". Morgan managed to have Thomas Lynch recalled to England, and a dissolute young peer, Lord Vaughan, succeeded him. He endeavoured to carry out the king's instructions to suppress piracy, but found that Morgan was conniving with the buccaneers behind his back. Morgan was deprived of his post as lieutenant governor and spent the remainder of his life in the grog shops he had permitted to open during his reign. He died in 1688, a shadow of his former self, and was buried near Gallows Point, Port Royal.

On 7 June 1692 an earthquake shook the island, and much of Port Royal was swallowed by the sea. At this particular time Port Royal had 2000 houses with 3000 resident inhabitants and a large floating population of soldiers, sailors, buccaneers and slave dealers. A contemporary account by the rector of the parish described his flock as "desperately wicked" and the population generally as "a most ungodly and debauched people".

Another account of the earthquake appeared in *The Gentleman's Magazine* of 1750:

> It happened on [the] 7th, just before noon and in the space of two minutes it shook down, and drowned, nine-tenths of the town of Port Royal. The houses sunk outright 30 or 40 fathoms deep. The earth opened and swallowed up the people in one street and threw them up in another; some rose in the middle of the harbour and yet were saved . . . Ships and sloops in the harbour were overset and lost . . . All this was attended with a rumbling noise, like thunder.

> The earth heaved and swelled like the rolling bil-
> lows ... In many places the earth crack'd, open'd
> and shut, with a motion quick and fast and of these
> openings two or three hundred might be seen at a
> time; in some of these people were swallowed up, in
> others they were caught by the middle and pressed to
> death, and in others the heads only appeared, in
> which condition dogs came and ate them ... scarce a
> planter's house or sugar-work was left standing in all
> Jamaica.

Morgan was the last of the old-time buccaneers. Those who came after him were simply pirates. Men like Edward Teach (alias Blackbeard), Steve Bonnet (the "Gentleman" pirate from Barbados), "Calico Jack" Rackman and others were never as important internationally as those who went before them were. Calico Jack would probably have been unheard of but for his association with Ann Bonny, the Irish pirate.

Most of her exploits were recorded by a Captain Charles Johnson in his *General History of the Pyrates*, published in London in 1742. Johnson had attended her trial and described it four years later in a preface to the book:

> As to the lives of our two female Pyrates [the other
> being Mary Read], we must confess they appear a
> little extravagant, yet they are never the less true for
> seeming so, but as they were publickly try'd for their
> Pyracies, they are living Witnesses enough to justify
> what we had laid down concerning them: it is certain
> we have produced some Particulars which were not
> so publickly known, the Reason is, we were more
> inquisitive into the Circumstances of their past Lives,
> than other People who had no other Design than that
> of gratifying their own private Curiosity: If those are
> some Incidents and Turns in their Stories which may
> give them a little the Air of a Novel, they are not

invented or contrived for that Purpose, it is a Kind of
Reading this Author is but little acquainted with, but
as he himself was exceedingly diverted with them
when they were related to him, he thought they might
have the same Effect upon the Reader.

Ann Bonny, sometimes spelt Anne Bonney, began life in
Cork, the illegitimate daughter of a Cork barrister. Her
father became involved in some intrigue against George I
and had to flee Ireland, taking his fifteen-year-old daughter with him to Charleston, South Carolina. Here he set up
a practice and prospered. Soon he bought a plantation and
became a rich man. His daughter, from descriptions of the
period, was a beautiful girl, but wild and wilful. She fell in
love with a handsome sailor named James Bonny, who
turned out to be a pirate. He smuggled her aboard a pirate
ship commanded by Jack Rackham, known as "Calico
Jack" because of his bright calico apparel. Ann was
dressed in man's clothing to disguise her sex and Rackham
taught her the art of wielding a cutlass and the use of a pistol. Ann Bonny tired of her husband, left him and fell in
love with another sailor on board who, to her amazement,
turned out to be a woman, Mary Read. She too had led an
adventurous life, having fought as a man beside her husband in the Seven Years War. When he was killed she took
to piracy, being a crack shot and an expert with the cutlass.

Ann Bonny then turned her affections to Captain Jack
Rackham. She took part in many of his engagements and
killed her first man before she was twenty. After a period
of about two years, Rackham's ship was boarded by a
party from a Royal Naval sloop. Rackham was drunk at
the time and put up little fight. In a court which tried the
whole crew, it was stated that Mary Read and Ann Bonny
were the only two who put up a fierce resistance to the
naval mariners. Both were pregnant at the time of their
trial and because of this could not be sentenced to death.
Mary Read died in childbirth, but Ann Bonny was eventually reunited with her father and faded from history.

Philip Gosse's book *The Pirates' Who's Who* recorded other incidences of Irishmen becoming pirates. Two other Irish pirates who infested the Caribbean were brothers from Cork, Andrew and Pierce Cullen. While passengers on a ship bound for Barbados in 1721, they took over the vessel, killed those of the crew who refused to join them and sailed to the Caribbean to become pirates. History does not record their eventual fate.

Another Irishman, named Richard Holland, rose through the private ranks to become captain of a large ship captured from the Spanish in 1724. His crew consisted of sixty Spaniards who chose to join him rather that be butchered; in addition, eighteen Frenchmen and eighteen Englishmen also chose to join him in the life of piracy.

One Darby Mullins from Londonderry became an orphan, and at eighteen years of age was sold to a planter in Barbados. Like Greaves, he managed to escape, and he joined the notorious Captain Kidd. He was eventually captured and hanged in New York in 1701.

Perhaps the sentiments expressed by one pirate, Bartholomew "Black Bart" Roberts, expresses the view of all pirates, escaped slaves or freemen: "In an honest service there is thin rations, low wages and hard labour; in this [i.e. roving], plenty and Satiety, pleasure and ease, liberty and power; and who would not balance creditor on this side, when all the hazard that is run for it, at worse, is only a sour look or two at choking [i.e. hanging]. No, a merry life and a short one shall be my motto."

CHAPTER FIFTEEN

The Irish and the Quakers

"To be fair, one should add that this situation disturbed some whites, notably the Quakers, who adopted a less compromising posture on slavery . . ."
Lerone Bennett Jr, social historian

IN AN AGE of intolerance and bigotry against the Irish, the attitude of the Quakers in Ireland and the West Indies shines out like a beacon in the darkness. The Quakers, or to give them their proper name, the Society of Friends, was founded by George Fox in 1648 in a small Leicestershire village. Soon, because of Fox's charismatic presence and the vigour of his teaching, the movement spread throughout England and Ireland. The Friends' beliefs were entirely at variance with the established religions of the day. Fox and his followers renounced all forms of ostentation in dress and manner and refused to fight or even to wear swords. Because the Almighty was so powerful a presence in their lives, they only uncovered their heads in their meeting houses, as they called them, and refused outside them to doff their hats to any man. They also held that all organised religions were leading men astray from the true worship of God. Their belief that God was not to be found in the preaching of ministers often led

189

them to interrupt church services when they claimed that they were moved by the Lord to do so.

Their converting, or "convincing" as they called it, soon attracted a large following, and Fox travelled throughout England setting up meetings, convincing people wherever he went. The new religion of self-expression which he preached could not be tolerated by the civil authorities. They received their nickname when George Fox, while he was being tried in Derby for preaching sedition in 1650, told the magistrates to "tremble at the name of the Lord". This phrase struck a chord, and the Society of Friends was henceforth often known as the Quakers.

The Quakers suffered terrible persecution at the hands of magistrates and judges, being publicly flogged, tortured and imprisoned with common criminals for prolonged periods of time. In 1653 two Quaker women, Mary and Elizabeth Fisher, were flogged in public in Cambridge. Their founder, George Fox, was thrown into prison in Leicester in 1654. On his release, Oliver Cromwell sent for him, doubtless anxious to discover what new sect had sprung up to plague him. He already had serious problems with the Baptists, a Protestant sect founded early in the seventeenth century, which held that baptism should be administered only to believers, and that it should be done by total immersion. One of its tenets was that infants should not be baptised, a tenet totally at variance with Protestant belief at the time. Cromwell "solved" the problem of the Baptists by shipping them to Ireland, there to be dealt with by his son Henry.

In his *Journal* Fox gives an account of this meeting:

> After some time Captain Drury brought me before the Protector himself at WHITEHALL. When I was came in, I was moved to say, "Peace be in this house" and I exhorted him to keep in the fear of God, that he might receive wisdom from Him, that by it he might be directed, and order all things under his hand to God's glory. I spoke much to him of truth, and

much discourse I had with him about religion, wherein he carried himself very moderately. But, he said, we quarrelled with priests, whom he called ministers. I told him, "I did not quarrel with them, but they quarrelled with me and my friends."

The Quaker doctrine soon spread to Ireland, although not to the Irish at first, but to the Cromwellian officers and soldiers stationed there. The first Quaker in Ireland was a William Edmundson, who had once been a soldier in the Cromwellian army. On his discharge, he was given a tract of land and farmed for several years. On a visit to England in 1653, he was convinced and returned to Ireland as a minister. His first convert was his brother, still serving as a trooper in the Cromwellian army. A short time later he convinced the governor of Londonderry and Colonel Nicholas Kempston, who provided land in County Cavan for Edmundson and other Quakers to settle in. Another important man whom he convinced was a Captain William Morris, who was, in Edmundson's words, "an Elder among the Baptists in great Repute, Captain of a Company, Justice of the Peace, Commissioner of the Revenue, Chief Treasurer in that Quarter, also Chief Governor of Three Garrisons".

In 1655, Edmundson was joined by two fellow Quakers, Edward Burrough and Francis Howgill. A few days after their arrival in Dublin, Howgill received a "call" to go west. Newly arrived in Ireland, he must not have been too sure of his geography, as he went south to Cork. He later described it in a letter "To all the Brethren in or about Kendal" that "a Colonell of the Protectors Army came to Dublyn . . . and desired any of us to goe with him into the County of Cork . . . I went along with him into the heart of the Nation about 50 miles from Dublyn through deserts Woods and Boggs and desolated places . . . without anie inhabitants Except a few Irish Cabins here and there who are robbers and murtherers that lives in holes and boggs where none can passe."

They broke their journey at a town which Howgill called Burrye, a garrison town where the colonel inspected the troops stationed there. After staying six days, during which Howgill convinced many of the garrison, they travelled on to Bandon, which Howgill described as a "great town . . . twelve miles below Cork near the sea", and where the colonel lived in a "gallant habitation" outside the town. The colonel invited the garrison and people of Bandon to his house on the afternoon of their arrival where the "gates would be open to all". Howgill reported that there came a "pretty deal of people" and appointed the following day for another meeting. At this meeting, Howgill said that some who attended "were a dark people, the offscourings of the English".

From Bandon, Howgill went to Cork, accompanied by Colonel Cooke and his wife. Here he met Colonel Robert Phaire, the governor of Cork. He describes Phaire as "a moderate man", although this is the Phaire, who, a couple of years earlier, helped Lord Broghill to round up and transport to Barbados 250 Irish men, women and children. Howgill had some success in convincing "captains and majors and officers" and held many meetings in the garrisons. He also states that "the priests are all in a rage".

He then travelled from Cork to Kinsale, where he was met and entertained by the governor, Major Richard Hodden. "The Governor, one Hoddyn, received me with his wife gladlie, and there is a greate fortress upon the sea Coast and on the first day [he] caused the Drumm to be beat, and all his souldiers called together and there came some people out of the Towne, soe there was a great meeting . . ." Howgill after his success in Kinsale returned to Bandon, where he held another great meeting. There were now meetings in private houses at Bandon, Kinsale and Cork. Colonel Cooke's wife in Bandon became one of the outstanding Irish Quakers.

Quakerism also spread throughout Munster. The Grubb family of Tipperary was convinced and did much to spread the message in that county. John Grubb had fought in Ireland and had been given a castle and 100 acres as a reward. He was convinced on a visit to England and returned to Cashel to preach the gospel there. The husband and wife did much to help the Irish among whom they lived, taking in the children of the poor and hiding them from the "man-catchers". They started a linen trade and employed Irish workers. In August 1656 John and Mary Grubb went to Waterford, Youghal and Cork and convinced many people there.

Many of the Quakers left Ireland and went to the West Indies, particularly to Barbados. William Penn, whose father had taken part in the Western Design, was convinced while at college in Oxford and later left for America, where he founded Pennsylvania.

Naturally, Henry Cromwell, as major general of the forces in Ireland, was deeply disturbed by the activities of the Quakers. He wrote to Thurloe on 6 January 1666:

> Our most considerable enemy in our view nowe are the quakers, whoe begin to growe in some reputation in the county of Corke, their meetings being attended frequently by Col. Phaier, Major Wallis, and moste of the chief officers thereabouts. Some of our souldiers have bin perverted by them, and amongst the rest his highness's cornet to his owne troop [Edward Cooke], is a professed quaker, and hathe writte to me in their style. Major Hodden, the governor of Kinsale is, I feare, goeing that way; he keeps one of them to preach to the souldiers. I think their principles and practises are not verry consistent with civil government, much less with the discipline of an army. Some think them to have noe designe, but I am not of that opinion. Their counterfeited simplicitie renders them to me the more dangerous.

Even before he wrote to Thurloe, Henry Cromwell had taken measures to crack down, hard and brutally, on the

Quakers. As early as December 1655, he ordered that all Quakers were to be arrested. All Quaker officers of whatever rank were to be discharged with ignominy. Men like Cooke, Hodden, Lieutenant Mason, his deputy governor, and other officers in Kinsale, Bandon and Cork were not only kicked out of the army, but some were arrested and gaoled. Colonel Cooke was imprisoned for three months without a trial. The amazing thing about these persecutions was that some of the officers had been appointed to their posts by Oliver Cromwell himself and were "old Ironsides", having fought with him in England, Scotland and Ireland. The 141 soldiers who had also served with him and who had become Quakers fared even worse than their officers. Many were discharged from the army without pensions, flogged and imprisoned for periods of up to six months for refusing to give up their Quaker beliefs.

The women Quakers fared no better. Lucretia Cooke, Colonel Cooke's wife, was twice imprisoned in Kinsale, once "for speaking a few words to the Priest and people", and another time for "desiring to speak to the chief Magistrate there about the Prisoners". Susan Michael was imprisoned in Cork for speaking to a priest in the steeple-house (a Puritan meeting place), as were two other women, Jane Tadpoole and Mary Gregory, for a similar offence.

The persecution spread to other parts of Munster. Colonel Henry Ingoldesby, a fervent Puritan who hated the Quakers, "set forth a Proclamation in Limerick . . . that no Inhabitant of the City should receive any Quaker into their house, upon Penalty of being turned out of the Town".

Two Quakers, a Captain James Sicklemore and John Perrot, who had been "convinced" by Edward Burrough in Waterford, were arrested in less than half an hour after their arrival in Limerick, "because they were met [with some inhabitants of Limerick] at the house of one Capt. Wilkenson". They were imprisoned for some days, and when Perrot asked for permission to preach in a steeple-house, he was beaten up and banished from the city.

John Perrot's story is a prime example of the zeal that caused the Quakers at the time to suffer imprisonment, torture, floggings and banishment. There is some doubt about Perrot's antecedents, although it has been claimed that he was the illegitimate son of Sir John Perrot, who was governor of Ireland in the latter part of the sixteenth century; Sir John himself was reputed to be the natural son of Henry VIII. The names Perrot or Parrott were found in many parts of Ireland and England in the sixteenth and seventeenth centuries.

The Perrot family was living about two miles outside Waterford when John was "convinced" by the two Quaker missionaries, Edward Burrough and Francis Howgill. Perrot, who had a wife and two young children, quickly took up the call to go out and convince others. Old letters exist in the library of the Friends' Meeting House in London written by Burrough, in which he states that Perrot "hath been much with me of late, & he hath been at many Steeple houses, he was Eminent in the Nation, & is a pretty Man".

Perrot travelled throughout Ireland, "a labourer in the gospel of Christ Jesus", as he put it. He again returned to Limerick and was again arrested by Colonel Henry Ingoldesby. This was the same Ingoldesby who, one year later, sentenced a Daniel Connery, landlord of Clare, with his three daughters, "beautiful girls" as they were described by Sir William Petty, who witnessed the trial, to slavery in Barbados. Their father was accused of harbouring a priest.

On Perrot's release, he then went to Kilkenny where he pleaded the case of 120 Roman Catholics held in gaol there awaiting transportation to Barbados. Perrot persisted in his efforts to get them all released. He outlined the difficulties in a letter to the pope:

> With the said Governor I pleaded (for the said persons) first, in his private house, and next, with him, and all the Commissioners, in the open Court of

Justice, who obtained a Warrant for the delivery of the said Prisoners, which I went personally to see executed; but the Marshal, hoping to gain Moneys, disobeyed it; which made me go a second time to the Court, and open the Cause afresh, whereby I obtained my Desire as full as I could possibly expect; for with a second Order I returned to that Prison (not giving trust to any human eye besides my own) and saw them all delivered.

The captives, when released, apparently fell on their knees in the street "worshipping" him, as he himself wrote, as if he were a god. He reproved them saying, "Thou shalt worship God, and Him only shalt thou worship."

Perrot now made it part of his mission to relieve the sufferings of the Irish during the years 1655 and 1656. He succeeded in obtaining the release of many other Irish Catholics awaiting transportation to Barbados from gaols in Waterford and Cork. The letter to the pope goes on:

Besides, other times I have appeared for some poor Widows, being formerly of eminency and repute in the World, and thy Children, and many other Roman Catholicks in their distresses; and God Almightly knows that the Pitties of my soul were such to them all, that I was so far from expecting a gift for all I did for them, that besides my Expenses in several Journies to serve their needs, my hand was open to all, and not one of thy children can say he came to my Door for an Alms, and went away empty-handed. Besides all this, the God of Knowledge remembers that I have stript off the Apparrel immediately from my body to cloath thy children that I saw in need and want.

Burrough and Howgill were expelled from Ireland in 1656, and Perrot was then left as the only Quaker minister and "Publisher of the Truth". He continued with his work of helping the Irish, and in this he must have had friends in high places, and although they never met, he and Henry Cromwell were in correspondence on several occasions. This probably saved him from the fate that befell many of the Quakers in England, but he was gaoled and beaten "with rods", as he termed it, in Kilkenny, the same gaol from which he had rescued the 120 Irish destined for Barbados. His mission in Ireland now drew to a close as a number of the "convinced" took up his work there. He left Ireland for England on 9 May 1656.

After a short stay in England, Perrot and a fellow Quaker, John Luffe, got the crazy idea of going to Rome to convince the pope. Perrot, on his arrival there, got in touch with a fellow Irishman, John Crey, who was chaplain to the pope. Crey tried to persuade Perrot that the mission was impossible, but the latter persisted. A couple of days later he was arrested and with Luffe was sentenced to three years imprisonment, not in a regular prison, but in a "mad-house", as Perrot described it. Luffe died while in prison, and Perrot was released before the end of his sentence, through the intervention, it was said, of Charles II. Perrot, on his return from Rome, found himself the centre of attention and spoke at many meetings in the south of England. Large crowds followed him wherever he went, impressed by his piety, humility and past sufferings for "the truth".

A short time later a quarrel broke out between Perrot and George Fox on what became known as the "question of the Hat". All Quakers refused to doff their hats to any man and uncovered only in the meeting houses. Perrot, going one further, said that as God sees all, there was no necessity to doff their hats to Him in the meeting houses. The quarrel split the Quakers down the middle and continued for many years. Because of it, Perrot decided to leave England and sailed from Gravesend in 1662 bound for Barbados.

When Perrot and his other Quaker friends arrived in Barbados, they found a Quaker community which had been in existence for six or more years, as Kenneth L. Carroll describes it in his biography, *John Perrot* (1970).

The first Quakers had come to Barbados in 1655 and Barbados then became "the cradle of American Quakerism". After preaching and convincing many there, some travelled on to carry the message to North America. Elizabeth Harris went to Maryland (probably in 1656), Mary Fisher and Ann Austin to Boston in 1656, and others to Virginia.

Those among the planters who were convinced welcomed Perrot, whose work in Ireland and Rome was known to them. On 3 November 1662, he wrote of the response he found on the island: "And now surely I can say the blessings of God are on Barbados, beholding that abundance of simple and single Love that I see, feel, and enjoy in the hearts of the simple, one towards another."

Many of the planters were rich men who owned many slaves, black and white. One of them, John Rous, whose son became a Quaker, changed the status of his white slaves to indentured servants and treated them well. Perrot convinced many of the other planters and prevailed on them either to free their white slaves or at least to make them indentured servants. As such, they were permitted to attend the Quaker meeting houses.

After spending some time in Barbados, Perrot travelled to Jamaica. He must have spent some time there, as he reported that the number of convinced people in Jamaica had doubled in the time he had been on the island. As ever, his chief interest was in the welfare of the Irish, and he begged all the settlers there who were convinced to ease their lot by cutting short their indentures or setting them free. Tireless in his endeavour to carry the message of Quakerism, he travelled from Jamaica to Maryland and Virginia, where he founded many meetings.

Early in 1664 Perrot was back in Barbados. Here he met and impressed Thomas Modyford, the governor, with his "great Cunning, searching and industrious Spirit", as well as "his good Temper, skill and knowledge in Merchant affaires". It was after this meeting with Modyford that Perrot forsook the Quaker rules about simple dress and not carrying weapons. As Modyford wrote to Charles II, with obvious satisfaction: "And really Sir it may take off much of the rude roughness of that Sects temper, when they shall find in the Newes bookes that John Perrot an eminent preachinge Quaker was Content for his magesties Service to appeare in a Sattin Sute with a Sword and Belt and to be Called Captaine."

Perrot's donning of the "Sattin Sute with a Sword and Belt" led him to be labelled a schismatic by Fox and his followers in England. Modyford appointed Perrot as a diplomat and sent him to Santo Domingo, capital of Hispaniola, to negotiate with the president general of the island on all good correspondence and commerce "between Jamaica and the Catholic islands".

Perrot used his influence with Modyford to better the state of the Irish Catholic white slaves and servants and obtained permission for them to attend meeting houses and take part in worship. (At one time Rous permitted his black slaves to attend the Quaker meetings, but this was forbidden by Governor Modyford.) Perrot's love and compassion for them never wavered, despite his harsh treatment in Rome. There is no record of the number of Irish that Perrot convinced, as the records were lost in the great fire in Bridgetown in 1670. A few of their names are listed among the Quaker archives in the library of the Friends' Meeting House in Euston Square in London. In return for his services in Santo Domingo, Modyford gave him a 300-ton ship to transport between 300 and 400 indentured servants to Jamaica. Perrot ensured that the majority of them were Irish. They became free men on their arrival.

It was the last service he performed for the Irish. A few months later, on 7 December, he died in Jamaica. He was buried, not in a Quaker cemetery, but, according to a contemporary, "in an old Popish mass-house". It was a fitting tribute to a man who had done so much for the enslaved Irish.

CHAPTER SIXTEEN

The Restoration and its Aftermath

*"[T]he Irish in the Reare (allwaies a bloody and perifidious
people to the English Protestant Interest) . . . fired Vollyes into
the ffront and killed more (then ye Enemy) of our owne
fforces . . ."*
Francis Sampson in a letter to his family (1666)

THE RESTORATION OF Charles II in 1660 raised the
hopes of the Irish, both at home and in the colonies,
that the millennium had come. Many of the indentured servants in Barbados, whose indentures were completed but who had not been given the land that had been
promised in their indentures, travelled to the island of
Montserrat were they found employment among their fellow Irishmen. Montserrat had been planted mainly by
Irishmen in 1632, invited there by the first governor,
Captain Anthony Briskett, himself an Irishman. They had
travelled there as free men and were given smallholdings
of between twenty-five and fifty acres apiece for tobacco
cultivation. We have few records of their early years as
these were destroyed by fire. It is also probable that some
of the Irish slaves who escaped from Barbados made their
way to Montserrat. We do have a record of the raid by the
French on the island in 1666, when the French attacked all

the English colonies in the Leeward Islands. They were eagerly joined by the Irish, both freemen and indentured servants, and did much damage to English property. After the island had been retaken by the English, the French who were captured were repatriated, but those of the Irish who were caught were immediately hanged. However, it would seem that many escaped and continued to wreak havoc on the English inhabitants.

In a petition, a group of "Loyall subjects of the Island of Mountserratt" wrote "To his Excellency William Lord Willoughbye":

> Wee with all other of his Majesty's Loyall subjects of this Island have so much above any other of our neighbours beene devastated wasted and destroyed in the late unhappye Warr, not only by our Ennymes in the tyme of their short staye with us, but have like-wise then as many tymes since a most barbarous and unhumane manner been Robbed, Plundered Stripped and allmost utterly Consumed of all that wee had in ye world by a Party of Rebellious and wicked people of the Irish nation or neighbours and Inhabitants in such sort, as it is allmost Impossible either for man or penn to utter or describe . . .

Lord Willoughby described Montserrat in 1668 as being "almost an Irish colony". The Irish, he said, had sworn to be true to His Majesty "and I believe them till an enemy appear". As late as 1676, a planter on the island said that the inhabitants "are mostly Irish, the better sort English . . . These two nations accord not upon this island. The Irish are most malicious against the English."

St Kitts, an island divided between the French and the English, was also attacked. The French were extremely jealous of the English prosperity in their part of the island. A French writer of the seventeenth century compared the English and French colonies in St Kitts. When Europeans first came to the island, he says, they lived in huts, and some lived in huts made by four or six forked branches stuck in the ground with walls of reeds and roofs thatched with palm or plantain leaves; but most then lived in houses of timber, stone or brick. The English had the best houses, which were generally well furnished, and more of them were married and did not live single lives as the French did. The sugar mills were made of wood. Those "who were able to hire people to oversee their Servants and Slaves, and to See that they do their work, lead pleasant lives, and want not those enjoyments thereof which are to be had in other countries ... They endeavour to outvye one the other in their entertainments ... All are taught the use of arms, and the Heads of Families seldom walk abroad without their swords."

The Irish indentured servants did not, however, enjoy the good life of their masters. These were miserably paid. In addition to board, lodging and clothing, they received for four years' service an amount of sugar valued at £1 17s. 6d. They were badly treated, being flogged for the slightest fault, real or imaginary. In light of such treatment it is not surprising that the Irish joined their co-religionist French.

Antigua, which was settled in 1632 with Edward Warner as governor, was also attacked by the French, who looted it and destroyed whatever property they could not carry away. The islands of Nevis and Barbados were not attacked on this occasion, but even in those islands the expense of the war was a strain. The whole militia were put on standby every night as the French privateers blockaded the coasts of Barbados.

Later in 1667 the English position was improved by the arrival of some naval reinforcements at Barbados under the command of Captain (afterwards Sir John) Berry. After a raid on Dutch shipping at Tobago, Berry sailed to the Leeward Islands with an expedition recruited and fitted out at Barbados. Off Nevis he defeated a combined French and Dutch fleet. After this victory Nevis was safe, and

Antigua and Montserrat were recaptured. St Christopher (St Kitts), however, was too strongly held to be attacked. Other expeditions were mounted and came to nothing until the war was brought to an end by the Treaty of Breda in the latter part of 1667.

In Ireland the disappointment in the Restoration was even greater than in the colonies. Very few of the landlords transplanted ever had their lands returned. On his arrival in London, Charles proclaimed that the Catholic rebels of 1641 were still traitors. The members of the Catholic Confederacy, who had fought so hard in his father's cause, were disowned by him. He again appointed Lord Ormonde as the new lord lieutenant of Ireland. Charles, for political reasons, promoted leading parliamentarian officers: Monck was made Duke of Albermarle and Lord Broghill, whose persecution of the Irish was legendary, was now one of his closest confidants. The local Cromwellian officers in Ireland, responsible for the transportation of thousands of Irish men, women and children, were reappointed to their positions as justices of the peace. An act, called the Act of Indemnity and Oblivion, was quickly passed through Parliament, granting indemnity to most of the former parliamentarians, with the exception of regicides. It soon became known as the Act of Indemnity for the king's enemies and Oblivion for his friends. Only those royalists who had joined Charles in exile, Ormonde, Taaffe, Inchiquin, O'Neill and a few others, retained their titles and got their lands back.

In Ireland it was estimated that seven eighths of all Irish Catholic landlords had been dispossessed by Cromwell; few of them ever got their lands back, and most of those who did received only a small portion of their former estates. Of the Irish who applied for restoration of their lands, 707 were declared innocent and deserving to have their lands restored; of these, 556 were Catholics. These were but a small fraction of the claims lodged and which were never satisfied. In July 1664 another act was passed in the Irish Parliament which returned to Catholics 22 per cent of the country, as opposed to the 59 per cent they held in 1641.

In Ulster there was no restitution of confiscated land; consequently the Tories, savagely suppressed by Cromwell, sprang into life again. They carried on a guerrilla war in Ulster, led by a distinguished former landlord and soldier, Count Redmond O'Hanlon, until he was betrayed and killed. Others took his place, men like Patrick Fleming and Rory O'Neill. As in the days of Cromwell, they raided the Protestant settlements, plundering, killing and driving off cattle. No Protestant landlord was safe in his bed. The military sent in pursuit of them adopted the Cromwellian tactics of fining the whole population of an area where an attack took place.

The authorities also resorted to Cromwell's old policy of transportation. During the 1660s, large numbers of Tories were "barbadoed", or sent to Jamaica. We know this because the viceroy of Ireland, Berkley, gave permission to Archbishop Plunkett to negotiate with them, offering thirty-seven of their leaders free pardon and transport out of Ireland to France or Flanders. In September 1670, fifteen accepted his offer, including Patrick Fleming, their leader, but instead of sending them to either of the continental countries, the government broke its word and sent them as slaves to Barbados.

The disturbed situation led to a continual harassment of the Catholic population, particularly in Ulster and Connaught. The Catholics who took no part in the activities of the Tories were placed in a quandary. The Tories raided their houses for food and forced them to contribute money and clothing. Then the military raided the self-same houses, plundering their homes and killing their cattle as revenge for attacks on them. In many cases the owner of the house was arrested and transported to Barbados. Four innocent Catholics were tried in Dungannon, accused of "corresponding with the Tories" and, after a mock trial, were publicly executed as a warning to others. Even the clergy were not immune. Five priests in County Tyrone were gaoled for no other reason than the disturbed state of their parishes.

During the second half of the seventeenth century, the clergy were ordered by their bishops to condemn the Tories in their parishes and to warn the faithful not to give aid to any Tory passing through their area. Archbishop Plunkett played a dominant part in the synods condemning the Tories, yet he understood the causes that drove landless men to try to regain their properties by force: "It truly moves me to compassion to see high families of the house of O'Neill, O'Donnell, Maguire, MacMahon, Maginnis, O'Cahan, O'Kelly, O'Ferrall, who were great princes till the time of Elizabeth and King James, in the memory of my father and many who are yet living; it moves one to compassion, I say, to see their children without property and without maintenance and without means of education."

Archbishop Plunkett himself was later arrested on the orders of Lord Ormonde. He was accused of high treason and charged with plotting, together with Bishop Tyrrell and a Colonel James Fitzpatrick, to bring a French army to Ireland. He was tried in Westminster Hall in London, and after evidence by several priests deeply antagonistic to the archbishop, was found guilty after a jury was out for only fifteen minutes, and executed.

The Irishmen on whose behalf Archbishop Plunkett had appealed and who were sent to Barbados were the last recorded group of Irishmen to be sent there. Englishmen were barbadoed by Judge Jeffreys after the suppression of the Monmouth rebellion (1686), as were Scotsmen after the rebellions of 1715 and 1745, but these are not the subject of this book.

CHAPTER SEVENTEEN

The Red Legs of Barbados

*"In the West Indies today, the poor whites survive in the Red
Legs of Barbados, pallid, weak and depraved from in-
breeding, strong rum, insufficient food and abstinence for
manual labour."*
Dr Eric Williams, former prime minister of Tobago and
Trinidad (1944)

TODAY BARBADOS IS unique among the colonies in
having a group of about 400 white men, women
and children concentrated in the parish of St
Andrews below St John's Church in the north-east of the
island: they are believed to be the last of the descendants
of the Irish and Scottish slaves and are known by the
derogatory title of "Red Legs". The reason for this is
obscure, but it is believed that it was first applied to the
Irish and Scots when they reached Barbados wearing their
kilts. Their legs were soon burned by the sun. Today, Red
Legs are of a sallow complexion and subject to many diseases like epilepsy, hookworm and anaemia.

They look down on the blacks and have never intermarried with them, and because of over 300 years of
inbreeding, many are now mentally retarded with a low
literacy rate. Through the years Scottish pride and Irish

stubbornness have helped them to maintain their independence, working small plots of land, growing a few provisions such as yams, potatoes, green peas and keeping a few chickens. They are also excellent fishermen, but only catch enough for their own needs.

The term "Red Legs" was first mentioned in 1798 by Dr J.W. Williamson, a fellow of the Royal College of Physicians in Edinburgh, who had served for some time in Jamaica and who visited Barbados on his way back to England. He wrote: "A ridge of hills, about the middle of the island, is called Scotland, where a few of the descendants of a race of people, transported in the time of Cromwell, still live, called Red Legs. I saw some of them, tall, awkward made and ill looking fellows, much of a guadroon colour, unmeaning, yet vain of ancestry; as degenerate and useless a race as can be imagined."

Other visitors to the island in the nineteenth century also described the living conditions of the Red Legs. Dr John Davy, inspector general of army hospitals in Barbados from 1845 to 1848, refers to the Irish and Scots as:

Poor Whites or Red Legs . . . Their hue and complexion are not such as might be expected, their colour resembles more that of the Albino than that of the Englishman when exposed a great deal to the sun in a tropical climate; it is commonly of sickly white, or light red, not often of a healthy brown; and they have generally light eyes and light coloured sparse hair. In make they bear marks of feebleness, slender and rather tall, loosely jointed, with little muscular development. In brief their general appearance denotes degeneracy of corporal frame, and reminds one of exotic plants vegetating in an uncongenial soil and climate.

Perhaps the best physical description of the Red Legs was made by Quintin Hogg when giving evidence before the West Indies Royal Commission in 1897:

> Then there are in Barbados . . . a certain number of so-called "mean whites—Redlegs", they call them . . . and so far from getting black they get bloodless in appearance and the sun have given to those parts of the body exposed to it a colour which finds its expression in the local name of "Redlegs" . . . It is a most pitiable thing to see them wandering about with some of the conceit of the white blood, but none of the energy of the European.

Not all the Red Legs resided in the district of Scotland in Barbados. Some drifted to Bridgetown in search of work, but this was impossible to find as black labour was cheaper, and apparently the blacks were more industrious, as the following quote, written by a young man of eighteen years who was living in Barbados with his father at the beginning of this century, shows:

> Of all the classes of people who inhabit Bridgetown, the poor whites are the lowest and most degraded; residing in the meanest hovels, they pay no attention either to neatness in their dwellings or cleanliness in their persons . . . I have never seen a more sallow, dirty, ill looking and unhappy race; the men lazy, the women disgusting; and the children neglected; all without any notion of principle, morality or religion; forming a melancholy picture of living misery; and a strong contrast with the general appearance of happiness depicted on the countenances of the free black, and coloured people, of the same class.

H.N. Coleridge, who visited Barbados in 1825, reported: "The lower whites of the island are without exception the most degraded, worthless, hopeless race I have ever met with in my life. They are more pressing subjects for legislation than the slaves."

Peter Simmonds, in a report for the Ministry of Education entitled "'The Red Legs', Class and Color Contradictions in Barbados", published some time before

I arrived in Barbados, wrote (he has very kindly allowed me to use extracts from it):

> In a cultural matrix where skin color and race are determinants of socio-economic rank, the "Red Legs" contradict the correlation. For though white skinned, they are economically impoverished and are considered a socially inferior underclass. Pushed or lured out of the British Isles over 300 years ago, they are uneducated, downtrodden, and powerless. Today, their ancient hopes denied, they are fading into oblivion and extinction as a homogeneous group, believing that they have been the cursed victims of the Lord's Will...
>
> Poor whites became synonymous with drunkenness and laziness, and many more were driven from their subsistence plots for failing to cultivate them. Harassed by the plantocracy and despised by the African slaves, they dispersed and settled in small groups near the arid eastern coast where they have remained on the fringe of Barbadian society.

Patrick Roach in his book *The Bridge Barbados* (1976) tells a story of Sir Winston Churchill's encounter with some Red Legs.

> Some years ago Lord Avon (previously Sir Anthony Eden) purchased "Villa Nova" a lovely old estate home located on a hill not far from St John's Church and while he was living there it is rumoured that he took Sir Winston Churchill, who was visiting Barbados at the time, driving through the Martin's Bay area and then along the East coast of Bathsheba. During this drive they encountered a few of the "Red Legs" and Sir Winston is said to have told Lord Avon that he considered it an absolute shame that the Royalists in England had permitted such poverty to exist amongst descendants of the old Royalist families who had been exiled or had to flee to Barbados during Oliver Cromwell's reign.

Of course, there are no royalist descendants among the Red Legs. As explained in the previous chapters, their ancestors either joined the militia before Barbados was taken over by the parliamentarians, or had been granted free pardons when Charles II ascended to the throne in 1660.

But the question remains: how did these descendants of Irish and Scottish stock settle in this particular area? To find the answer one has to go back to the Emancipation Act of 31 July 1834, which proclaimed slavery abolished. If emancipation meant complete freedom for the slaves, it was certainly not the case in the colonies. The Assemblies in all the colonial countries bitterly opposed it, feeling that it was imposed on them by the House of Commons. Men and women were still needed on the plantations to cultivate the sugar cane. In order to make the transition from slavery to freedom smoother, the act stipulated that all slaves were to be apprenticed to the planters who owned them, and the period of apprenticeship was to run until the 1 August 1840, six years later.

It was back to the old form of indentured servitude, but with this difference: the apprentices were still regarded as slaves by the planters. There were special terms written into the act; for instance, all children under the age of six were to be immediately freed, but in the event of such children becoming destitute (and at that age they naturally would be) they were to be apprenticed to the planter to whom the mother was apprenticed. A child of twelve was apprenticed to a planter until he or she reached the age of twenty-one. The act also stipulated that all the apprentices were to be fed, clothed and given medical attention. All these points, needless to add, were honoured more in the breach than in the observance.

The apprentices, for their part, were required to work honestly, not to show any insolence or insubordination and to observe all the terms of the contract strictly. It was slavery under another name. The apprentices naturally resented having to do the same work as they had done as slaves. The planters, acutely aware of the six-year expiry date, worked their apprentices harder than ever. The whip could still be used, usually for insubordination or for staying away from work. If an apprentice missed work for two days running, he was sentenced to twenty lashes on the bare back; if for three days he received thirty-nine lashes. For insubordination, an apprentice was sentenced to fifty lashes and three months in prison. Female apprentices were not supposed to be flogged, but planters got around this by declaring before a magistrate that a female had been insubordinate, whereupon she was automatically given the statutory fifty lashes and three months' imprisonment. While in prison women could be flogged on the slightest pretext for allegedly poor work, or for refusing to gratify the sexual desires of the warders.

The magistrates almost always sided with the planters. They were poorly paid and received rich rewards from them. At that time, sugar still accounted for 97 per cent of the total exports of Barbados, and the labour of apprentices was essential to the island economy. The white property owners wanted to preserve their privileges in local government, in business, in the Assembly and in the Council. They still possessed the Big Houses and still had the apprentices at their beck and call.

One cannot tell, after the passage of over 350 years, whether the Irish white slaves felt equal, if not superior, to the blacks. Despite what Colonel John Scott had written about the relationship between the Irish and the blacks ("They are . . . a very great part Irish, derided by the Negroes"), it is an undisputed fact that the Irish played a dominant part in many of the slave rebellions. Six years after the passing of the Emancipation Act, they were thrown into a direct conflict with the blacks in a search for jobs.

Planters, forced to hire workers for the first time, found the blacks demanded lower wages and were more docile and hard working. The poor whites were regarded as arrogant, drunken and lazy. A letter in one of the newspapers blamed alcoholism for their state: "Their present condition and use may be briefly summed up in the statement that they act as so many sponges to soak up our rum, and by a curious process of melting down of thews and sinews, (to say nothing of moral qualities) to augment the nett proceeds of our distilleries."

One member of the Poor Relief Commission said that as well as their excessive consumption of alcohol, they were morally and possibly intellectually degenerate. In contrast, he stated, they were simultaneously persons of extreme arrogance. Certainly I found these two traits—alcoholism and arrogance—much in evidence when I managed to interview two of the Red Leg community during my research on the island.

The Red Legs were harassed by the plantocracy and despised by the newly freed black slaves. They retreated and settled in small groups near the arid eastern coast, where their descendants remain today. Their situation was made worse by their inability to mix with either the white planter class, who make up only 5 per cent of the population of Barbados today, or with the 95 per cent black population.

CHAPTER EIGHTEEN

The Red Legs Today

"Certain there are many Catholic families in Ireland today who count it among the proudest memories of their history that some representative of their name was sold in the West Indies."
Reverend Aubrey Gwynn, "Cromwell's Policy of
Transportation" (1930–31)

BARBADOS TODAY IS a holiday island, intent on shedding its colonial past. I flew there by jumbo jet, taking ten hours for the journey. I picked up one of the glossy in-flight magazines and read: "Historical, cultural and architectural buffs can satiate their appetites for Barbados heritage with a wide selection of great houses that provide excellent insight into the life and times of the early settlers of the island." Just that.

I very much doubted that many of the passengers in the plane were history buffs. I am sure that few of them, English, Irish or Scots, knew or cared that some of their countrymen made that journey in stinking sailing ships 350 years ago, ships that took ten or more weeks to cover the same distance we were covering in as many hours.

After sleeping off my jet lag in one of the good but relatively inexpensive hotels in the west of the island, I telephoned Mrs Betty Carrillo Shannon, who immediately invited me to the Barbados Museum and Historical Society. I found a charming, literate lady in a building that was once a British garrison gaol. She informed me that she had had many enquiries from overseas about the fate of Scottish and English prisoners transported there by Cromwell and later by Charles II. She had received only one enquiry about Irish prisoners, from a Mr Carroll of Bantry, County Cork. I was the first Irishman to visit with the specific purpose of writing a book about them. She ushered me into the reading room. It contained shelves full to bursting point with books on West Indian history, and on the floor were dusty files which looked untouched for many years.

Mrs Shannon fixed an appointment for me with a Barbadian of Irish descent, who had written a book on Barbados which included a chapter on the Red Legs. Next day, I met Patrick Kelman Roach, who was to be my mentor and guide during my stay on the island.

Patrick Roach is a direct descendent of one of two brothers, John and James Roach, who went to Barbados from Limerick in 1638 and obtained a plot of thirty acres from the then governor, Henry Hawley. They first went into tobacco growing, but when that failed promptly changed to sugar growing. In this they prospered, marrying first cousins. One of the brothers became a sugar merchant dealing with buyers in London and Liverpool. To their credit they, together with a few Irish planters, did their best to alleviate the sufferings of their fellow countrymen transported by Cromwell. P.K., as he was known to everybody, was a tall and very fit man of seventy, his blue eyes betraying his Celtic heritage. His book *The Bridge Barbados* gives an interesting account of the island's history.

In a chapter on the Red Legs, he wrote:

> Living in Barbados today there are approximately four hundred people derisively called Red Legs, or Poor Bakros or Scotland Johnnies. These descendants of prisoners or emigrants who came to Barbados

have a history which goes back to around
1660 ... The name Red Legs or Red Shanks, as they
were called many years ago, dates back to when these
people arrived in Barbados. Many of them were
wearing kilts and, of course, their legs had been
burned red in the unaccustomed sunshine.

The name Poor Bakro was given them because,
although they were Christians and were permitted to
go to the same Church as their owners, they were
only allowed in the back rows and, of course, this
was a cause for the black slaves to deride them.

P.K. pointed out that in his book he was referring to
Scottish Presbyterian prisoners of war. The Irish, being
Catholics, were not regarded as Christians by the
Protestant planters and were not allowed the solace of any
religion. This may explain why so many of those with
Quaker masters became "convinced" Quakers.

Peter Simmonds in his report gives a fuller explanation
of the term Bakro or Buckra as he calls it:

> To illustrate, Buckra is a word in common usage in
> West Africa meaning "white man", but in plantation
> Barbados it was recycled and came to mean not just
> any white man, but specifically, the white man in the
> back row, the traditional place of worship for the Red
> Legs. Ecclesiastical stratification was a straight reflec-
> tion of secular stratification. The Church house on
> Sunday reflected the daily organisation of the social
> hierarchy;—white planters in the pews closest to the
> altar, if not to salvation; then the white petite bour-
> geoisie (plantation functionaries such as overseers,
> book-keepers, etc.); then the black petite bourgeoisie
> (the local school masters, civil servants, etc.,); then
> the black folk, and in the pews closest to the door, the
> Red Legs—poor white Johnnies in the back row.

P.K. showed me a document in the library which,
although it did not refer to Barbados but to Jamaica,

217

shows the religious bigotry of the time. It was a preface to the first published collection of the *Laws of Jamaica* in 1683, written by a Francis Hanson, and read: "We have very few Papists, for neither Jesuits or Non-conformists Parsons do or can live among us; some few have attempted, but never could gain Proselytes enough to afford them sustenance (though all except Papists may freely exercise what religion they please without disturbance)."

What was true of Jamaica was also true of Barbados. Joseph J. Williams, SJ, in a book named *Whence the "Black Irish" of Jamaica* (1932), wrote: "It is only natural to suppose that the bulk of the early Irish in Barbados and Jamaica must have lost the faith within a generation or two."

In his book P.K. expressed great sympathy for the Red Legs of Barbados:

> The food handed out to the Red Legs in the last year of their indentureship was steadily reduced and, of course, they died like flies. Only those survived who originally must have been very strong physically and mentally. If they complained they were flogged. If they worked badly they were flogged. If they worked well they were forced to do twice as much. Under conditions of this sort, it is understandable that the human body would suffer from continual malnutrition and tension. Eventually they became resigned to fate and gave up fighting for better conditions.

Simmonds sums up by giving a sample from a catalogue of views held by members of society:

> Red Legs were said to be lazy, worthless drunks of unworthy origin, who had neither ambition nor intelligence, yet were white and proud; they were said to have squandered what little they ever had and deserved their current fate; they were reaping their just desserts from the Lord for drinking too much and not working to earn their keep, and the sooner

they died off the better for society and themselves; they were also said to smell and to be dirty. One white petit bourgeois intellectual summed them up thus: "Pride and prejudice produces poverty. This is the classic example, my dear boy."

On the accusations of laziness:

One of the long-time accusations hurled at the Red Legs is that they are lazy and do not like to work. Whereas they may be work-shy in terms of employment in a straight master/servant, employer/employee bifurcation, any aversion to manual labor evaporates in a self-employment or communal situation. Respect for land is profound. An informant said: "What I would like before the Lord take my life would be a bigger piece of ground. When I see what people doing with the land these days, it is a shame. If I could get some I would show dem. You see my little piece and you know that I ent do too bad. Show how the times change. In days gone by every little piece of ground had something growing pun it. But people get worthless." Recalling how conditions on the plantation had changed, he said: "I remember how years ago I used to work for 60 cents a day; now I getting $7.20 a day. In the old days they used to make me work real hard in the field but now it is only light work and I getting $7.20 a day."

Simmonds goes on to describe the conditions of the Red Legs of today:

For most Red Legs, life in a poverty culture provides almost no opportunities for fun and frolic. Most seldom laugh because there is seldom reason to laugh. For them life has been a humorless drag and the problematics of keeping body and soul together seem to have drained them of even the wish to laugh. They are removed even from that situation where people reach

219

a level of cynicism where they laugh at themselves. But there are exceptions. One of my informants likes to have fun and enjoy himself. He was one of the centers of attraction at a village fete, drinking his rum, dancing, and singing some ancient calypsoes. When I button-holed him he was rum-soaked and too happy about the fact to care; "My boy, I had plenty fun. My boy, I behave pissy! You know pissy? I get on like I make myself. You does only live once and dead once and the way I feel tonight, I could be dead tomorrow." He chided those who never found it possible to have a good time and predicted: "Some of these people 'bout here who don't drink, nor smoke, nor screw nobody, bound to go mad. That could never happen to me. Rum never make nobody mad yet."

I have quoted Peter Simmonds, a highly educated man of mixed racial background who is married to a white woman, at length because he has a better understanding and insight into the Red Legs' mentality than any other person I encountered in Barbados.

During my stay in Barbados, I was introduced by P.K. to a few of the descendants of the planter class living there today. They make up only 5 per cent of the total population but are inordinately proud of their ancestry and despise the black government. One comment which I heard at the Barbados Yacht Club was, "They have the government, old boy, but we have Broad Street." What I think he meant was that they had the financial muscle, owning most of the principal shops and stores in Broad Street, Bridgetown's Mayfair. I should hasten to add that there are a few exceptions. One friend of P.K.'s, Ronald Taylor, seemed to number black politicians and businessmen among his friends. The original Taylor, also named Ronald, came out with Courteen and became a rich planter and member of the Assembly.

During my stay, I accompanied Ronnie Taylor and P.K. to the churchyard behind St John's in the parish of St Andrew's.

There stands the tomb of Ronnie's ancestor. A huge domed edifice, it was blocked by slabs of concrete. Ronnie, who was about seventy, pointed to it and remarked, "They will have to open it one day for me." Ronnie's maternal ancestor was a Browne from Galway. The Reverend Aubrey Gwynn, in his article on "Cromwell's Policy of Transportation" (1930–31) mentions a Colonel Browne who was the subject of correspondence between Thurloe and Monck. Apparently he was buying up Scots as soon as they landed and shipping them back by return to Scotland.

On our way back to Bridgetown from St John's, we passed through the area where most of the Red Legs settled. P.K., who was driving, slowed down but did not stop to speak to any of the inhabitants. When I asked the reason, P.K. said, "They are a very reclusive people, Sean, and do not like being approached by strangers."

However, I did make contact with two Red Legs. My first contact, Benny, who claimed to be of Irish descent, said he was fifty-five years old, although he looked nearer seventy. Toothless, bald with a sallow complexion, he wore a pair of jodhpurs and a tweed jacket which covered a filthy undervest. He wore no socks but had on a pair of sneakers through which his bare toes protruded. All the clothes were second or third hand, patched and torn. On his head he wore an ill-fitting English-style tweed cap with a greasy peak. It was a remarkable outfit for the middle of August, but the heat didn't seem to bother Benny.

I met him in one of the low-class grog shops so prevalent in Bridgetown. It was crowded at ten o'clock in the morning, with some of its habitués already drunk and snoring quietly. The heat was oppressive, the small fan in the corner fighting ineffectually to circulate the hot, stale air. Benny's drink was rum and during our session he put away almost three quarters of a bottle of it. He couldn't understand why I didn't drink; all white men in Barbados drank.

He began by telling me of his early life on a small plot of land in the Red Leg area which was situated in the north-east section of the island. Life was hard there. He had five brothers and five sisters, none of whom ever went to school. The family subsisted off the small plot, although his father often fished, and on a good day brought home enough to feed the whole family. His father was a drunkard, and when Benny found half-empty bottles after his father had passed out, he drank the contents, so that by the age of eight, he confessed proudly, "I was a drunkard, too." His mother, worn out by hard work and childbearing, died when he was ten. His eldest sister, then aged thirteen, took her place as head of the household and as her father's "second wife", as Benny put it. He ran away from home at the age of thirteen because he could no long stand the drunken beatings his father administered to all the family.

He came to Bridgetown and obtained a job as a washer up in a restaurant. Here he found unlimited opportunities to drink, and Benny fully availed himself of them. He also availed himself of the black girls who worked in the restaurant. It was patronised by white men, and Benny was often asked where they could find "a young, clean coloured girl". By the age of eighteen, Benny was a full-time pimp, engaging not only black girls but white Red Legs, including three of his own sisters. His life from then on became rum, his stable of girls and fights with fellow pimps. He still bears the scars from some of them.

Eventually he became too old for "the job", as he described it. Younger, more violent men took over. He now subsisted on the earnings of one young black woman with whom he lived. He had no regrets for the past. "De Lord he sends, and de Lord he takes away" was his philosophical comment as we parted.

While in Barbados I attended an Anglican service at St John's Church. The sparse congregation was black and a black minister took the service. In a couple of rows at the back were a few Red Legs, easily distinguished by their features. When the service was over, I approached one of them and introduced myself. This was a well-dressed boy of about twenty-one or so, with fair hair and vivid blue eyes. Except for his sallow skin he could easily have passed for an Irishman, attending mass on Sunday.

He was obviously uneasy in my presence, but gave his name as John Curtin. I remarked that Curtin was an Irish name and asked if he could give me any information about his forebears. He replied that his father and grandfather were born "down there", pointing to the ridge of hills below the church. This was as much as he knew of his family's background. He and his father were fishermen and also worked on their plot of land. He had been to school until the age of twelve, then left to join his father. "I must go now to join my friends." He turned and left abruptly.

Later I asked a senior police officer to whom I was introduced if there was much crime in the Red Legs' community. "None," he answered; "at least none that is ever reported to us. They keep to themselves and settle their problems among themselves. The only time we have problems with them is when they leave their community and settle in Bridgetown. The young girls are often forced into prostitution by the pimps who prey on them. Then there are knife fights among the pimps who run them." I asked if drug addiction was a problem in the Red Legs community. "Again, no," came the reply. "Of course, we know that they grow cannabis, but shut our eyes to that. The only people they are harming are themselves . . . and," he added after a pause, "I do not believe that smoking cannabis does much harm, anyway."

Have the Red Legs any future? According to Peter Simmonds, in his conclusion to the report he presented to the Ministry of Education, they have none as a viable community. He sees miscegenation and education as the only solutions. "Watching the children of Martin's Bay and its environs making their way to school each morning, it was clear that two active solutions were already at work—miscegenation between rural working-class blacks and Red Legs, and compulsory education. Born with a brown skin and armed with a basic education, these children shall never know what it really means to be a Red Leg."

In a novel published in 1971 and called *One Touch of Nature*, Barbadian writer Lionel Hutchinson puts forward a similar solution. He advocates marriage into the black middle class and goes on in the novel: "This would ensure a triadic sharing of the spoils: the father would achieve what may have been a life-long ambition by marrying a woman who could 'raise the children's color' and probably raise his standing in the eyes of his peers; the mother would be hijacked from the confinement and stigmatization of life 'under the hill'; and the child shall have the protection of a brown skin."

Apparently "under the hill" means residence in the Red Legs settlement under Newcastle Hill, while "going up the hill" means "upward mobility", leaving the settlement and gaining social recognition and acceptance outside the confines of the settlement.

My friend P.K. Roach mentioned two families which made it "up the hill" in the last half century. The Mayers became successful businessmen while two of the Goddards became highly respected doctors. Another brother, John Goddard, became a chartered accountant, captain of the West Indies cricket team and a racehorse owner. Two families in fifty years. What of all the others still living "under the hill"? They never intermarried with the blacks in 350 years. Will they do so today?

Father Williams in his book *Whence the "Black Irish" of Jamaica* (1932) describes how the Irish there were assimilated into the black population and became known as the "Black Irish". Only time will tell. In Barbados today there are hundreds of black families with Irish names: O'Connors, O'Carrolls, O'Dowds, O'Duffys, Fitzgeralds, Fitzpatricks, etc. These are the descendants of the Irish who married black women during the plantation days. While I did not come to Barbados in search of "roots", I did not find an O'Callaghan or a Callaghan among them.

The usual explanation given for the presence of Irish names is that indentured servants and slaves took the family name of the planter who owned them. This is patently ridiculous, as in the list of assemblymen in Barbados, I found only two Irish names, Barry and Browne. In the list of landowners there were four: Lynch, Nugent, Roach and Fitzgibbon. I did not get close enough to any Red Legs to find out if any bore that name.

The days before leaving Barbados, I made one last effort to contact them. I took a hotel taxi and toured the north and east of the island. Passing through the Red Legs settlement "under the hill", I saw young white girls peering shyly out of doorways, then quickly turning aside as I attempted to photograph them. When I stopped, a group of scowling men advanced threateningly, hoes and pitchforks in their hands. The black hotel driver panicked and we drove off. P.K. Roach was right; they do not welcome the attention of strangers.

On our return journey we passed the only house in Barbados still standing from early plantation days. It is St Nicholas Abbey, the only stone house built during the period and still occupied, although not by the descendants of the planter who built it. The slave lines have long disappeared and a fine lawn covers the ground where the ancestors of the Red Legs lived in squalor and degradation. How many of them lie buried in unhallowed ground or were thrown into the nearby swamps, now filled in? The waving sugar cane still grows there, "thick as a man's wrist", as Ligon described it.

It was a melancholy outing, and although I was glad to get back to the gaiety and bustle of the hotel, I could not get the Red Legs out of my mind. Perhaps somebody, somewhere will do something to ease their plight. It is my fervent hope that Catholic families in Ireland who, according to Reverend Aubrey Gwynn, "count it among the proudest memories of their history that some representative of their name was thus sold in the West Indies", will band together and do something for their long forgotten brethren—the Red Legs of Barbados.

BIBLIOGRAPHY

The material contained in this book was gathered from several sources.

1. Barbados

Much information was obtained from unpublished documents in the Library of the Barbados Museum and Historical Society and from old records in the Barbados Archives. Many of these documents have not been catalogued.

"Acts of Assembly Passed in the Island of Barbados 1648–1717", *Journal of the Barbados Museum and Historical Society.*

Anonymous, *Barbados: Memoirs of the first Settlement on the Island of Barbados*, Barbados Museum and Historical Society, 1741.

Barbados Museum and Historical Society, Letters and Documents appertaining to early life in Barbados.

"The Voyage of Sir Henry Colt, Knight, to the Island of the Antilles", *Journal of the Barbados Museum and Historical Society*, XXI, No. 1.

2. London

The Public Records Office at Kew in London contains the State and Colonial Papers for the period. They have much information on ships sailing from ports in England and Ireland, giving the names of masters, ships' captains, and in some cases, the number of persons transported during the period in question.

Acts of the Privy Council (Colonial Series).

Calendar of State Papers (Colonial Series, America and West Indies), 1541773, 27 vols. London: 1862–1939.

Calendar of State Papers (Domestic) 1649–1700.

Calendar of State Papers (Irish Series).

3. Books and Articles

Abrahams, P. *Jamaica: An Island Mosaic*. London: 1957.

Alleyne, Warren. *Caribbean Pirates*. London: 1986.

Andrews, K. *The Western Enterprise: English Activities in Ireland, The Atlantic and America (1480–1650)*. Liverpool: 1978.

Barbour, P.L. *The Three Worlds of Captain John Smith*. London: 1964.

Beakles, H. *White Servitude and Black Slavery in Barbados 1627–1715*. Knoxville: 1989.

Bennet, George. *The History of Bandon and the Principal Towns in the West Riding of County Cork*. Enlarged edition. Cork: 1869.

Bennett, Lerone Jr. *The Shaping of Black America*. New York: 1974.

Blome, Richard. *A Description of the Island of Jamaica*. London: 1698.

Bromley, J.S. *Corsairs and Navies: 1660–1760*. London: 1987.

Bruce, Philip A. *The Economic History of Virginia in the Seventeenth Century*, 2 vols. New York: 1896.

Buchan, John. *Cromwell*. London: 1970.

Burke, Edmund. *An Account of the European Settlements in America*. London: 1770.

Burke, T.N. *Lectures*. New York: 1872.

Burns, A. *History of the British West Indies*. London: 1954.

Campbell, P.F. *Some Early Barbadian History*. Bridgetown, Barbados: 1993.

Carleton, C. *Going to the Wars*. London: 1992.

Carlyle, T. *Oliver Cromwell's Letters and Speeches*. London: 1894.

Carmen, H.J. and Syrett, H.C. *A History of the American People*, vol. 1 (to 1865). New York: 1952.

Carroll, Kenneth L. *John Perrot*. London: 1970.

Carroll, Kenneth L. "Quakers in the Cromwellian Army in Ireland". London: 1978.

Carroll, Michael J. *A Bay of Destiny*. Bantry, Co. Cork: 1996.

Carte, Thomas. *A History of the Life of the Duke of Ormonde*. London: 1735.

Carthy, J. Ireland. *The Flight of the Earls to Grattan's Parliament (1607–1792)*. Dublin: 1949.

Coward, B. *Oliver Cromwell*. London: 1991.

Craton, Michael. *Sinews of Empire: A Short History of British Slavery*. London: 1974.

Bibliography

Cusak, M.F. *A History of the Irish Nation*. London: 1874.

Dallas, R.C. *The History of the Maroons*. London: 1803.

D'Alton, Edward Alfred. *History of Ireland*. London: 1910.

Davies, J. *The History of the Caribby-Islands*. London: 1666.

Davies, K.G. *The North Atlantic World in the Seventeenth Century*. Minneapolis: 1974.

Davis, N.D. *The Cavaliers and Roundheads of Barbados 1650–1652*. Georgetown, British Guinea: 1887.

Dunlop, Robert. *Ireland Under the Commonwealth*. Manchester: 1913.

Dunn, R.S. *Sugar and Slaves*. London: 1973.

Eaden, J. (Ed.) *The Memoirs of Père Labat, 1693–1705*. London: 1931.

Earle, Peter. *The Sack of Panama*. London: 1981.

Ellis, A.B. "White Slaves and Bondservants in the Plantations", *Argosy*. Georgetown, British Guinea: 1883.

Emmet, Thomas Addis. *Ireland Under English Rule*. New York: 1903.

Firth, C.H. *The Narrative of General Venables*. London: 1900.

Fitzmaurice, E.G.P. *The Life of Sir William Petty*. London: 1895.

Foster, N. *The Horrid Rebelion in Barbados*. London: 1650.

Foster, R.F. *Modern Ireland: 1600–1972*. London: 1988.

Fox, Bourne H.R. *The Story of the Colonies*. London: 1869.

Fox, George. *Journal*. London: 1691.

Franklin, J.H. *From Slavery to Freedom: A History of Negro Americans*. 1967.

Fraser, Antonia. *Cromwell: Our Chief of Men*. London: 1973.

Esquemeling, J. *The Buccaneers of America*. London: 1925.

Frere, G.A. *Voyage to the Islands Madeira, Barbados, Nieves, St. Christophers and Jamaica*. London: 1707.

Gage, T. *The English–American: A New Survey of the West Indies*. London: 1648.

Gardner, William James. *History of Jamaica*. London: 1873.

Gaunt, Mary. *Where the Twain Meet*. New York: 1922.

Gookin, Richard. *A History of the Gookin Family*. Salem: 1991.

Gosse, Philip. *The Pirates' Who's Who*, London: 1924.

Gwynn, Aubrey. "Cromwell's Policy of Transportation", *Studies*, vol. XIX, no. 76, *Irish Quarterly Review*. Dublin: December 1930–June 1931.

Gwynn, Aubrey. "Early Irish Emigration to the West Indies 1612–43".

Gwynn, Aubrey. "The Irish in the West Indies, Analecta Hibernica", Irish Manuscripts Commission, vol. 4. Dublin: 1932.

Harlow, Vincent T. *A History of Barbados 1625–1685*. Oxford: 1926.

Holland, Rose J., Newton, A.P. and Benians, E.A. (Eds.) *The Cambridge History of the British Empire, vol. 1, The Old Empire from the Beginnings to 1783*. Cambridge: 1929.

Hull, C.H. (Ed.) *The Economic Writings of Sir William Petty*. Cambridge: 1889.

Hunte, G. *Barbados*. London: 1974.

Hutton, R. *Charles the Second, King of England, Scotland and Ireland*. Oxford: 1989.

Johnson, Charles. *General History of the Pyrates*. London: 1742.

Johnson, James Hugo. *Race Relations in Virginia and Miscegenation in the South*. Cited in Lerone Bennett Jr.

Jones, James. *Acts of the Assembly Passed in the Island of Jamaica from 1770–1793*. Kingston: 1786.

Kelley, A.M. *The Economic Writings of Sir William Petty*. London: 1963.

Lecky, W.E. *History of Ireland*.

Ligon, Richard. *A True and Exact History of the Island of Barbados*. London: 1657.

Long, E. *The History of Jamaica*. London: 1774.

MacGeoghan, Abbe. *History of Ireland, Ancient and Modern*. Dublin: 1844.

Marley, David F. *Pirates*. London: 1995.

McGee, Thomas D'Arcy. *History of the Irish Settlers in North America*. Boston: 1852.

McLaughlin, A.C. *A History of the American Nation*. 1899.

Mechan, Charles Patrick. *The Confederation of Kilkenny*. Dublin: 1882.

Murphy, Dennis, S.J. *Cromwell in Ireland: A History of Cromwell's Irish Campaign*. Dublin: 1885.

Newton, A.P. *European Nations in the West Indies*. London: 1933.

O'Donnel, Elliot. *The Irish Abroad*. London: 1915.

O'Fiaich, T. and Forristal, D. *Oliver Plunkett – Our Sunday Visitor*. Huntington, Indiana: 1975.

Bibliography

O'Rourke, Canon. *The Battle of the Faith in Ireland*. Dublin: 1887.

Parry, J.H. and Sherlock, P.M. *A Short History of the West Indies*. London: 1971.

Petty, William. *The History of the Survey of Ireland, commonly called the Down Survey*. London: 1719.

Petty, William. *The Political Anatomy of Ireland*. 1672.

Poyer, John. *The History of Barbados from the First Discovery of the Island*. London: 1808.

Prendergast, John Patrick. *The Cromwellian Settlement of Ireland*. Dublin: 1865.

Puckrein, G.A. *Little England: Planatation Society and Anglo-Barbadian Politics (1627–1700)*. New York: 1984.

Quyn, T. "The State and Condition of the Irish Catholics from the Year 1652–1656". (Quoted from *Studies* by Aubrey Gwynn, op. cit.).

Rinuccini, Giovanni Battista. (Quoted from *Studies* by Aubrey Gwynn, op. cit.).

Roach, P.K. *The Bridge Barbados*. Bridgetown, Barbados: 1976.

Schomburgk, R.H. *The History of Barbados*. London: 1848.

Scott, John. *A Description of Barbados*. London: 1667.

Sheppard, J. *The Red Legs of Barbados*. London: 1977.

Sherlock, P. *West Indian Nations: A New History*. Jamaica: 1973.

Simmonds, Peter. " 'The Red Legs', Class and Color Contradictions in Barbados". Bridgetown, Barbados: 1982.

Sloane, Hans A. *Voyage to the Islands*. London: 1707.

Smith, Emerson. *Colonists in Bondage, White Servitude and Convict Labour in America*. 1947.

Smith, John. *Generall Historie of New England, Virginia and the Summer Isles*.

Temple, John. *History of the Horrid Rebellion in Ireland*. London: 1646.

Thurloe, J. *A Collection of the State Papers of John Thurloe*, (Ed. Thomas Birch), 7 vols. London: 1742.

Wertenbaker, T.J. *Patrician and Plebeian in Virgina*. Charlottesville: 1910.

Whistler, H. *A Journal of a Voyage from Stokes Bay for the West Indies*. London: 1655.

Williams, Eric. *Capitalism and Slavery*. North Carolina: 1942.

Williams, Eric. *From Columbus to Castro, A History of the Caribbean 1492–1969.* London: 1972.

Williams, Joseph J. *Whence the "Black Irish" of Jamaica.* New York: 1932.

Woodbury, G. *The Great Days of Piracy in the West Indies.* New York: 1951.

INDEX

Act for Regulating Servants, 152

Act of Good Affection, 44–6

Act of Indemnity and Oblivion, 204

Adventurers, the, 45–6, 52

"Advertisements for Ireland", 162

Alderyne, Thomas, 95

America, and Irish slaves
  conditions of, 164–8
  indentured labour, 166–70
  racial mix, 164, 167–70
  transportation of, 161–4

Antigua, 148, 203, 204

Aran Islands, priests transported to, 64

Aston, Sir Arthur, 21, 23–4, 27

Atkins, Sir Jonathan, 108

Austin, Ann, 198

Avon, Lord (Anthony Eden), 210

Ayscue, Sir George, 28, 101

Baptists, 190

Barbados
  "cabbage stalk" soldiers, 136–7, 138–9
  cotton plantations, 89–90
  Irish names in, 224–5
  and Quakers, 193, 197–9, 217
  racial mix, 209–10, 212–13, 217, 224–5
  and "Red Legs", 207–13, 216–26
  settlement of, 65–70, 74
  sugar plantations, 90–3, 97–100, 102–9, 212
  tobacco plantations, 67–8, 89
  see also slave trade; slavery

Barbados Museum and Historical Society, 93, 216

Bate, Dr, 13, 19

Beckford, William, 109

Bell, Sir Philip, 70, 100

Bennett, George, 78

Bennett Jr, Lerone, 163, 164, 166, 167, 169, 189

Benny (Barbadian "Red Leg"), 221–2

Berkenhead, Mr, 135, 136, 137

Berringer, Benjamin, 102

Berry, Sir John, 203

Blackbeard, 181, 185

Bonnet, Steve, 185

Bonny, Ann, 185–6

Bonny, James, 186

Boscowen, Mr, 96

Bougchier, Sir Arthur, 162

Bradley, Arthur Granville, 153–4

Brennan, Denis, 59

Index

Brereton, Sir William, 15
Briskett, Anthony, 201
Broghill, Lord, 31, 32, 33, 81, 86, 192, 204
Browne, Colonel, 221
Bruce, Philip A., 167, 168–9
buccaneers, 171–85
  Irish, 154, 176, 185–7
  origins of, 171–2
Buchan, John, 36–8
Buckley, Thomas, 72
Burke, Edmund, 8
Burke, Reverend T.N., 85
Burns, Sir Alan, 175
Burrough, Edward, 191–2, 194, 195, 196
Butler, Sir Edmund, 28, 29
Butler, Elinor, 50
Butler, Gregory, 135, 137, 142
Butler, James see Ormonde, Earl of
Butler, Richard, 17, 19
Butler, Walter, 35, 38

cabbage stalk soldiers, 131–43, 146, 147
Campos, Pedro a, 65
Carlisle, James Hay, Earl of, 67, 68, 69, 99
Carlyle, Thomas, 15–16, 39
Carroll, Kenneth L., 198
Carroll, Michael, 216
Casas, Bishop Bartolome de las, 140
Cashel, sacking of, 16, 28
Castletownroche (Co. Cork), 47–8
Catholic Confederation, 17–18, 30, 35, 49, 204

Charles I, King of England, 11, 13–14, 16, 18, 67, 162
Charles II, King of England, 12, 18, 42–3, 158–9, 180, 182, 197, 201, 204
Charter of Barbados, 101–2
Chichester, Sir Arthur, 161
Child, Josiah, 73–4
children, slavery of, 79, 86, 103, 113, 148–52, 154, 211
Churchill, Sir Winston, 210
Civil War (England), 11, 14, 15, 93, 98
Clarendon, Earl of, 99, 100
clergy see priests, transportation of
Clonmacnoise Decrees, 33
Clonmel, siege of, 35–6
Clotworthy, Sir John, 79
Cole, John, 95
Coleman, Captain, 60
Coleridge, H.M., 209
Colt, Sir Henry, 69
Columbus, Diego, 140
Company of Royal Adventurers, 83
Comyn, Sir Nicholas, 49
Connaught, transplantation to, 44–53, 55–61, 77
Connery, Daniel, 195
Cooke, Edward and Lucretia, 192, 193, 194
Coote, Sir Charles, 18, 42, 45, 62
Coote, Chidley, 27
Council for Trade and Plantations, 108
Courteen, Sir William, 65–7
Craddock, Anthony, 71, 73

Index

Craton, Michael, 96
Crey, John, 197
Cromwell, Henry, 45, 153, 190
  and Quakers, 193–4, 197
  and transportation, 61, 79, 109, 145, 149–51, 152
Cromwell, Oliver, 11, 18
  campaign in Ireland, 19–25, 27–39, 41, 48
    Clonmel, 35–6
    Drogheda, 20–5, 27, 37–8
    Wexford, 28–30
  and Quakers, 190
  and transplantation, 45, 48, 52–3, 57–8
  and transportation, 61, 80, 81–2, 93, 145–9, 159
  views on Irish, 12–13, 14–15
  "Western Design", 131, 132–4, 139, 141–3, 153
Cuba, 133, 135, 140
Cullen, Andrew and Pierce, 187
Curtin, John, 223

D'Alton, Reverend E.A., 114–15
Daniell, Mr, 146–7
Davy, Dr John, 208
Deakins, Alice, 71
de Poincy, Chevalier Lonvilliers, 173
Desborough, John, 134, 135
Dickson, William, 104, 116, 117
Dillon, Lord, 35
Dominica, 125
Down Survey, 51–2, 81

D'Oyley, Edward, 142, 157
Drax, James, 99, 102
Drogheda, siege of, 20–5, 27, 37–8
Dugan, Sir Walter, 44

Earle, Peter, 174–5, 183
Eddis, William, 164
Edmundson, William, 191
Ellis, A.B., 8, 86, 93
Emancipation Act (1834), 211, 212
Emmet, Dr Thomas Addis, 79
Exquemelin, A.O., 173–5, 183–4

Fairfax, Sir Thomas, 11
Ferrall, Richard, 31–2
Fisher, Mary and Elizabeth, 190, 198
Fitzgerald family, 60
FitzNicholas, Thomas, 63
Fitzpatrick, Daniel, 59
Fitzpatrick, James, 206
Fleming, Patrick, 205
Foley, John, 60
Fontaine, Peter, 168
Forde, Father, 62
foreign armies, Irish in, 43–4, 61, 77–8, 81, 86
Foster, R.F., 85
Fox, George, 189–91, 197, 199
Foyle, Oxenbridge, 94–6
French, Dr Nicholas, 27, 29

Gage, Thomas, 131, 132–3, 140, 143
Gaunt, Mary, 151

Index

Goddard family, 224
Goodall, Richard, 123
Goodson, Vice-Admiral, 138
Gookin, Daniel (the
  Younger), 163
Gookin, Danyell, 162–3
Gookin, Richard, 163
Gookin, Vincent, 58–9
Gosse, Philip, 180, 187
Greaves, "Red Legs", 177–9
Gregory, Mary, 194
Grubb, John and Mary, 192–3
Gwynn, Reverend Aubrey, 9,
  51, 85–6, 215, 221, 226

Haiti *see* Hispaniola
Hanson, Francis, 218
Hardman, Daniel, 166
Harris, Elizabeth, 198
Haselrigge, Sir Arthur, 96
Hawley, Henry, 68–9, 101,
  124, 216
Herbert, Thomas, 33, 50, 63
Hetherington, Mr, 59
Higginbotham, Lieutenant
  Colonel, 124
Hispaniola, 133, 135, 137–9,
  172, 176, 199
Hodden, Richard, 192, 193,
  194
Hogg, Quintin, 208–9
Holland, Richard, 187
Howgill, Francis, 191–2, 195,
  196
Hughes, Neal, 72
Huncks, Henry, 69–70
Hutchinson, Lionel, 224

Ikerrin, Lord, 57–8
Inchiquin, Murrough

O'Brien, Lord, 16, 21, 28,
  30–1, 43, 204
indentured labour, 91, 93
  in America, 166–70
  conditions of, 73–6, 111–12,
    154–7, 166–9, 203
  contracts of, 70–1, 152, 164
  freed, 125, 201–2
Ingoldesby, Henry, 46, 194,
  195
Ireton, Henry, 19, 41, 50–1

Jamaica, 182, 184–5, 217–18
  buccaneers in, 172, 173, 180
  captured by English, 131,
    139–41, 142–3
  Irish slaves in, 148–57
  and Quakers, 198–9
  settlement of, 145–8,
    153–4
  sugar plantations, 145,
    148, 154, 182
James I, King of England,
  161, 162
Jeaffreson, Christopher, 128
Jeffreys, Judge, 206
Jepson, Colonel, 53
Johnson, Charles, 185–6
Johnson, James Hugo, 168
Johnson, John, 80
Jones, John, 123
Jones, Michael, 19, 23, 32
Justamond, 174

Kavanagh, Charles, 58
Keegan, Robert, 60
Kempston, Nicholas, 191
Kendall, James, 129
Kidd, Captain, 187
Kilkenny, siege of, 35, 38

Kinsale, 33, 71–2
Kipling, Rudyard, 175

Labat, Père, 103, 106, 112, 171–2
Lambert, John, 133
Lane, Reverend Thomas, 68
Lang, Andrew, 174
Laureus, Henry, 161
Lawrence, Colonel, 50, 55–7
Lecky, W.E., 13
Lenthall, Sir William, 96
Leslie, Charles, 154–5
le Vasseur, Monsieur, 173
Ligon, Richard, 65, 74, 75, 91–2, 97–8, 99, 102, 121, 179, 225
L'Olonnois, François, 176–8
Long, Edward, 151
Loughrea Commission, 46, 48, 49, 50, 55
Ludlow, Edmund, 132
Luffe, John, 197
Lynch, Sir Thomas, 157–8, 182, 183
Lyttleton, Charles, 157

MacMahon, Heber, 42
McMaster, J.B., 164
Maguire, Lord Conor, 14
Maracaibo, 183
Margarita, 179
Maryland, 165, 167, 169, 170, 198
Mather, Cotton, 181
Mayer family, 224
Mayo, Christopher, 44
Michael, Susan, 194
Milton, John, 133–4
Minshinogue, Dr, 53

Modyford, Sir Thomas, 97–8, 101, 102, 116, 136, 158, 182, 183, 198–9
Monck, General, 16–17, 158, 204, 221
Montserrat, 67, 137, 201–2, 204
Morgan, Henry, 181, 182–4, 185
Morgan, Thomas, 55, 61, 80
Morris, Catherine, 49
Morris, Lewis, 136, 137
Morris, William, 191
Mullins, Darby, 187
Murphy, Reverend Denis, 29
Muskerry, Lord, 44
Myngs, Commodore, 180–2
Mytton, Thomas, 15

Neterville, Father, 62
Nevis, 67, 137, 148, 179, 203
Newton, Captain, 84
Noell, Martin, 95, 96, 102, 106, 131–2, 133, 134, 136, 142, 146, 147
Norris, Sir John, 44, 63
North, Dudley, 80

O'Callaghan, Donogh, 49
O'Derrick, "Blind Donough", 51–2
O'Donnell, Elliott, 81–2
O'Hanlon, Count Redmond, 205
O'Moore, Rory, 14
O'Neill, Daniel, 42
O'Neill, Henry, 42
O'Neill, Hugh, 31, 35–6, 41–2, 43, 204

Index

O'Neill, Owen Roe, 17–18, 20, 42
O'Neill, Sir Phelim, 14, 44
O'Neill, Rory, 205
Ormonde, James Butler, Earl of, 11–12, 14, 16, 17, 18–19, 20–1, 22, 30–1, 35, 42–3, 179–80, 204, 206
O'Rourke, Canon, 16

Penn, William (elder), 134, 135, 139, 142, 145
Penn, William (younger), 193
Perrot, John, 194–9
Peters, Hugh, 19
Petty, Sir William, 51–2, 58, 59, 81, 195
Phaire, Robert, 192, 193
pirates *see* buccaneers
plantation owners, 97–100, 102, 106–9, 112, 116–17, 166, 169, 198
Plunkett (buccaneer), 179–80
Plunkett, Archbishop Oliver, 205, 206
Povey, Richard, 73
Povey, Thomas, 131, 132, 133, 134, 146, 147
Powell, Henry, 66
Powell, John, 66
Poyer, John, 147–8
Prendergast, John Patrick, 46, 82, 154
Preston, Thomas, 17
priests, transportation of, 61–4, 86
Puerto Bello, 183
Puerto Rico, 135, 140

Quakers
in Barbados, 193, 197–9, 217
beliefs, 189–90
in Ireland, 191–7
in Jamaica, 198–9
persecution of, 190, 193–5, 197
Quigley, Patrick, 165–6
Quyn, Reverend Thomas, 85

Rachman, "Calico Jack", 185, 186
Ramirez, Juan, 141
Read, Mary, 185–6
rebellion (1641), 13–14, 16, 17, 45
"Red Legs", 207–10, 219–26
history of, 211–13, 216–19
Rinuccini, Cardinal Giovanni Battista, 8, 17, 42–3, 77, 82–3, 85, 111
Rivers, Marcellus, 94–6
Roach, John and James, 216
Roach, Patrick Kelman, 179, 210, 216–18, 220–1, 224, 225
Roberts, Bartholomew "Black Bart", 187
Roche, Maurice, Viscount and Lady, 47–8
Rodney, Admiral, 107
Rous, John, 100, 198, 199
Rous, Thomas, 73, 100

St Kitts (St Christopher), 66–7, 137, 148, 173, 176, 202–3, 204
St Lucia, 125
Sampson, Francis, 201

Sankey, Hierome, 58
Santiago de Cuba, 180, 181
Scots, in Barbados, *see* "Red Legs"
Scott, John, 102–3, 112, 212
Searle, Daniel, 63–4, 101–2, 123, 125, 126, 127, 135, 137, 147, 158, 177
Sedgewicke, Robert, 142, 143
Shannon, Betty Carrillo, 10, 215–16
Sharpe, Horatio, 169
Sicklemore, James, 194
Simmonds, Peter, 209–10, 217, 218–20, 223–4
Sinnott, David, 28
slave trade, African, 80, 84, 86–7, 93
slave trade, Irish, 77–88, 159
  to America, 161–3
  auctions, 112–13, 119
  to Barbados, 25, 33–4, 52, 53, 59–61, 80
  children, 79, 86, 148–52, 154
  conditions during transportation, 73, 78–9, 81–5, 86–8, 95–6, 163
  earliest, 71–4
  to Jamaica, 147–52, 205
  numbers transported, 85–6
  priests, 61–4, 86
  prisoners of war, 93–4
  profits from, 79–80, 86–7
  slave ships, 79–80, 83–5, 86–8
  women, 77–8, 79, 81–2, 86, 109
  see also indentured labour; slavery

slavery, of Irish
  abolition of, 211–13
  in America, 161–70
  auctions, 112–13, 119
  children, 79, 86, 103, 113, 148–52, 154, 211
  conditions during, 74–6, 94, 102–6, 111–21, 154–7, 163–9
  plantation owners, 97–100, 102, 106–9, 112, 116–17, 166, 169, 198
  prejudice against Irish, 126–8, 137
  punishments, 118–19, 120–1, 124–9, 152–3, 165, 167, 212
  and Quakers, 197–9
  racial mix, 98, 102–3, 104, 114–17, 119–20, 164, 167–9
  rebellions, 123–9
  runaways, 123–9, 165–6
  stud farms, 115–16
  women, 77–8, 79, 81–2, 86, 109, 113, 114–16, 118, 119, 145, 167–9, 212
  see also indentured labour; slave trade
Sloane, Sir Hans, 152–3, 184
Smith, Abbott Emerson, 163–4
Smith, John, 162
Spenser, William, 48–9
Stackpool, Ignatious and Catherine, 49
Stafford, Captain, 28–9
Stafford, Brother John, 63

Index

Standing Committee for
   Jamaica and the West
   Indies, 147
Stokes, Luke, 148
Stubber, Colonel, 33
sugar plantations, 90–3,
   97–100, 102–9, 145, 148,
   154, 212
   conditions in, 74–6, 94,
      102–6, 111–21, 154–7,
      163–9
Swanley, Captain, 15

Taaffe, Sir Lucas, 30, 204
Tadpoole, Jane, 194
Taylor, Ronald, 220–1
Teach, Edward (Blackbeard),
   181, 185
Temple, Sir John, 13
Thomas, Dalby, 90–1
Thorpe, Mary, 50
Thurloe, John, 131–2, 145,
   148–9, 150–1, 193, 221
Tobago, 125, 203
Tories (outlaws), 51–2,
   55–62, 77, 80, 86, 159,
   177, 205–6
Tortuga, 172–3, 176, 177,
   178, 180
transplantation, to
   Connaught, 44–53, 48–50,
   55–61, 77
transportation see slave trade
Trapham, Dr, 156–7
Tufton, Sir William, 67–8
Tuite, James, 60
Turner, Murtagh, 59

Tyrrell, Bishop, 206

Vaughan, Lord, 184
Venables, Robert, 134–6,
   137–8, 139, 141, 142, 145,
   146, 172
Verney, Thomas, 68–9
Vernon, John, 81
Virginia, 72, 74, 79, 80,
   161–4, 165, 167, 168, 169,
   198
Von Uchteritz, Heinrich, 94

Warner, Edward, 203
Warner, Sir William, 66–7
Waterford, siege of, 31–2
Wertenbaker, T.J., 164
West, Joseph, 71–3, 91
Wexford, siege of, 28–30
Whetstone, Sir Thomas, 180,
   181–2
Whistler, Henry, 97
White, Don Ricardo, 44
Whitelocke, Bulstrode, 14
Williams, Eric, 96, 109, 207
Williams, Joseph J., 218, 224
Williamson, Dr J.W., 208
Willoughby, Lord William,
   100–1, 127–8, 158, 202
Windsor, Lord Thomas, 157,
   158, 180–1, 182
Winslow, Edmund, 135, 143
women, slavery of, 77–8, 79,
   81–2, 86, 109, 113,
   114–16, 118, 119, 145,
   167–9, 212
   stud farms, 115–16

SOME OTHER READING

from

BRANDON

DONAL J. O'SULLIVAN

The Irish Constabularies
1822–1922
A century of policing in Ireland

This first account of the Irish constabularies is a major
contribution to Irish historical studies. Throughout the
century in question policing stood at the perilous
intersection of politics, religion and the relationship
between Britain and Ireland. Donal J. O'Sullivan has
over three decades researched this history, much of the
essential material of which had been obscured by
continuing political sensitivities.

From the Constabulary Act of 1822 and the organisation
of the County Constabulary, the story moves through the
difficult and turbulent decades of the Famine, 1848, the
Belfast Riots and the Fenian rising, encompassing the
birth of the Royal Irish Constabulary and the Land War.
In the later years of the nineteenth century the emphasis
is on more routine police work, with the period of the
growth of Irish nationalism in the early twentieth century
being a peaceful time for the RIC. But as Sinn Féin and
the Volunteers grew in strength, attitudes to the RIC
changed and it came under sustained attack during the
force's final difficult years leading to disbandment.

"An excellent overview of the roots of Irish policing."
The Irish Times

"A valuable contribution to the debate on the role of
policing in contemporary society." *Sunday Business Post*

"Fascinating." *Ulster News Letter*

ISBN 0 86322 257 9; Hardback £30.00

Francis J. Costello

Enduring the Most
The Life and Death of Terence MacSwiney

Terence MacSwiney's seventy-three-day hunger strike in Brixton prison in 1920 marked a turning point in Ireland's struggle for independence. His courage and purpose made a profound impression on Irish and world opinion, and still echo through Irish political life.

A member of the Provisional Government, Lord Mayor of Cork, and Commander of the Cork No. 1 Brigade of the IRA, MacSwiney was one of the leading republican activists of his generation. He was also a writer of plays and political works, including *The Principles of Freedom*, and left a body of writing that encompassed poetry, political philosophy and ideas for Ireland's economic development.

Francis J. Costello's biography, the first to have full access to the MacSwiney family papers, creates a rounded portrait of MacSwiney's character and beliefs. It explores his life in all its complexity, and is at once the story of one of history's martyrs and a record of Ireland's revolutionary years.

ISBN 0 863222 220 X; Paperback £9.99

JOE GOOD

with an introduction by Tim Pat Coogan

Enchanted by Dreams
The Journal of a Revolutionary

A fascinating first-hand account of the 1916 Rising and its aftermath, *Enchanted by Dreams* brings alive the historic events that ushered in the beginnings of an independent Irish state.

A Londoner and a member of the Irish Volunteers, Joe Good guarded the approach across O'Connell Bridge as the rebels took the centre of Dublin. He joined the garrison in the GPO, and describes at first hand the events of the insurrection: the confusion, the heroism, and the tragedy of Easter Week.

After the Rising Joe Good worked as an organiser for the Volunteers. He was a close associate of Michael Collins and his portrait of Collins provides fresh insight into his character, his competitiveness, and how he related to his men. In 1918 Good was one of a handpicked team sent to London to assassinate members of the British cabinet, and here he gives the first full account to be published of this extraordinary expedition. Joe Good, born in London in 1895, died in Dublin in 1962. He wrote his journal in 1946 for his son Maurice, who has now edited it for publication.

ISBN 0 86322 225 0; Paperback £9.99

DENNIS COOKE

Persecuting Zeal
A Portrait of Ian Paisley

"Stunningly insightful. . . well researched and attractively presented." *Fortnight*

"The Cooke 'report' on Paisley is reasoned and unemotional. But it is also daring in a place where sectarianism drives men to murder." *Observer*

"A rounded and authentic picture . . . an insight into the life and times of Ian Paisley that cannot but be of help to anyone trying to understand or ameliorate the lethal depths of sectarianism that have nurtured and still sustain Ian Paisley . . . A very valuable book." Eric Gallagher, *Methodist Recorder*

"In contemporary Ireland, no one has better exemplified the interlocking of the twin powers of politics and religion than the viciously anti-Catholic Ian Paisley. . . This highly qualified author writes with an admirable mixture of clarity, charity and scholarship ... I conclude with one word of advice: read this book . . . It is, literally, a tract for our times." Tim Pat Coogan, *Examiner*

ISBN 0 86322 242 0; Paperback £9.99

HELEN BRENNAN
The Story of Irish Dance

This is the first full account of the phenomenon of Irish Dance. Writing in a style that is authoritative but very accessible to the general reader, Helen Brennan traces the story back to the early account of dance customs in medieval Ireland. She focuses on the developments of the 19th century (with the introduction of quadrilles, waltzes, etc.), and explores how dance played a vital role in the formation of a new national culture.

A wealth of colourful anecdotes bring alive the surprisingly strong conflicts which arose in relation to dance – conflicts with puritanical church leaders; between native dancers and bureaucratic instructors; and over what constituted "real" Irish dancing.

In modern times there has been a revival of set-dancing, and there has been the enormous international success of *Riverdance*. Helen Brennan gives a lively and fascinating account of the many aspects of Irish dance today and yesterday.

"*The Story of Irish Dance* is of interest to the general reader and as a source for scholars of Irish dance, dance anthropology, folklore and cultural studies. It is a book well worth reading." *The Irish Times*

"Accessible and lucid . . . entertaining and stimulating." *Irish News*

ISBN 0 86322 244 7; Hardback £15.99

23rd November 2001